Digital Consumer Behavior

Digital Consumer Behavior

Navigating the Dynamics,
Building the Demand

Dr. Kyle Allison

BEP

BUSINESS EXPERT PRESS

Leader in applied, concise business books

Digital Consumer Behavior:
Navigating the Dynamics, Building the Demand

Cover design by Charlene Kronstedt

Interior design by S4Carlisle Publishing Services, Chennai, India

First published in 2025 by
Business Expert Press, LLC
222 East 46th Street, New York, NY 10017
www.businessexpertpress.com

ISBN-13: 978-1-63742-856-6 (paperback)
ISBN-13: 978-1-63742-857-3 (e-book)

Business Expert Press Marketing Collection

First edition: 2025

10 9 8 7 6 5 4 3 2 1

EU SAFETY REPRESENTATIVE
Mare Nostrum Group B.V.
Mauritskade 21D
1091 GC Amsterdam
The Netherlands
gpsr@mare-nostrum.co.uk

To Melissa & Bailey.
My hearts, purpose & world.

Description

Digital Consumer Behavior: Navigating the Dynamics, Building the Demand has one central focus for practitioners and students—become the expert to deliver ultimate digital consumer experiences at the synergy of qualitative thinking and quantitative execution. This book is perfect for anyone who wants to not only immerse themselves with foundational consumer behavior theories and concepts but also learn how it is applied with practical and applicable strategies for today's modern digital consumer.

With over two decades of experience leading digital strategy for some of the world's most influential retailers, the author expertly combines academic insights with hands-on expertise. As a trusted consultant and digital marketing innovator, the author has navigated the intricacies of e-commerce and digital business growth, bringing a wealth of knowledge to this guide.

This book simplifies the complexities of digital consumer behavior, breaking it down into actionable strategies. Readers will learn how to map the consumer journey, understand the psychological drivers of engagement, and implement advanced tactics to boost loyalty and drive conversions. The content is rich with case studies, strategic frameworks, and practical tips tailored for executives who need data-driven solutions and for students eager to master the art of digital marketing.

Digital Consumer Behavior empowers readers to thrive in a rapidly shifting digital environment, emphasizing the importance of delivering personalized and relevant consumer experiences. The author's proven methodologies have helped brands exceed their digital marketing goals—and, now, these insights are yours to apply.

Whether you're an executive focused on optimizing your digital approach or a student aspiring to break into the field, this book will deepen your understanding and equip you to build meaningful, lasting connections with today's digital consumers.

Contents

List of Figures

Preface

Modern digital business requires an even more profound understanding—one that brings academic knowledge closer to the practical challenges and potentialities we encounter every day. The goal of this book was my simplest, but most impactful goal: to provide a one-stop guide that is an amalgamation of what I've seen and heard about digital marketing and online business along with the fundamental principles of consumer behavior.

As a professional and professor who experienced the highest of highs and lowest of lows in digital strategy, I understand firsthand the skills gap in the market. Digital strategists and marketers are notoriously unable to reconcile qualitative thinking with quantitative thinking when considering the consumer experience. This chasm isn't an abstract idea—it's a practical issue that impacts the performance and success of online businesses. Expediting this gap requires something special, something that empowers practitioners to think big and implement data-driven strategies strategically.

I've also experienced this lack of unity in education. Consumer behavior classes teach foundational concepts, but the linkage to digital strategy is rarely covered or elaborated. I wanted to change that by making the connections between formal education and digital marketing practice. This book will not only educate but will also help you optimize your digital strategy and enable you to make accurate and informed readings of consumer habits.

CHAPTER 1

Exploring Digital Consumer Behavior

The best way to predict the future is to understand the present.
—Peter Drucker

Chapter Overview

Yesterday's consumer is not the same consumer as of today. Most understand this. The connectivity of technology and the capabilities of digital communications are impressive. The challenge for some companies, though, is understanding the consumer at the core of those advanced capabilities and at the crossroads of that immediate technological connection. So, before we can even strategize the consumers of tomorrow, it's important to grasp the true depiction of digital consumers today.

Starting Point

The consumer is in charge, period. Yes, that's right, the consumer in business today is the one dictating our markets, guiding our product development, shifting our marketing focuses, and positioning our brands competitively. It may be that we think we control our business, even with the best intent of doing the right thing for our consumers. The truth is we don't control much of it at all.

Sure, we can manage our budgets, dictate what we do in our digital marketing strategies, and decide how we approach connecting with our consumers. However, it is all in how we manage the simple notion that we are doing it at the mercy of what our consumers do, say, buy, and, ultimately, react to from those areas we think we can "control." For some, this may be a bold stance to take in and absorb, but if we do not at least acknowledge this up front, the ability to navigate the digital consumer landscape moving forward will be a challenge. So, let us take a pause, take a deep breath, accept it, and now move toward the good things we can do to connect, strengthen relationships, and, ultimately, build our business.

The Foundation

Digital consumer behavior varies in definition. For this book, digital consumer behavior *is the examination of consumers' interactions, touchpoints, influences, and decision processes in their online activities.* Assessing consumer behavior is multifaceted, especially online. The varying degrees of opportunities for consumers to find brands, engage with them, develop relationships, and advocate are vast and complex. This is where the focus on all elements of the digital consumer journey and experience matters. You must be able to focus on all elements with this foundation in mind.

The true meaning of consumer behavior is more about the *continuous learning* of your consumers than it is *about knowing.* You build the knowledge at a point in time, but digital consumerism is not static. The true nature of digital consumerism today regarding behaviors is dynamic and adaptive. This is the crux some digital marketers find themselves in when it comes to believing that they have a grasp of their digital consumers. Truthfully, the foundation of digital consumer behavior is that we only strengthen our knowledge through the advancement of lessons learned from those innovative digital strategies we conduct.

Emergence of Digital Consumerism

To appreciate where we are today in digital business, it is important to remind ourselves where we have come from. The number of worldwide Internet users alone, according to Meltwater (2024), has grown from 4.1 billion in 2020 to close to 5.3 billion in 2024. Projections indicate up to 8 billion users will have access to the Internet by 2029. The sheer connectivity and accessibility to the Internet have increased the reach for companies. The widespread expansion covering over 60 percent of the population of the world currently indicates no shortage of potential consumers to target for our digital marketing purposes.

However, more than access is needed. Focusing on the true growth of active online shoppers is a bit different but substantial. EMARKETER (2020) reported that, in the year 2025, the number of global online shoppers will rise up to 2.77 billion. This indicates that approximately one-third of the world's population has access to the Internet and shops online. It does not seem year-to-year growth in this activity will slow down anytime soon either, as more Internet providers seek to advance their accessibility, and more individuals gravitate toward online interactions, engagement, and shopping.

The Pandemic Effect

The onset of the COVID-19 pandemic significantly accelerated the e-commerce industry, prompting both frequent online shoppers and those who were loyal to physical stores to transition to digital platforms because of lockdowns and health concerns. This surge in demand prompted the emergence of direct-to-consumer (D2C) models and the rapid transition of numerous businesses to online operations. It also prompted innovations in supply chains. With the reopening of physical stores following the pandemic, a hybrid retail model was created by combining the convenience of online shopping with the in-store experience. The deeply ingrained e-commerce habits ensured the continued growth and evolution of digital shopping, even though in-person shopping made a comeback.

The pandemic resulted in a rapid and dramatic transition to online shopping, transforming a gradual change into an overnight revolution. In regions that were particularly hard hit, physical stores encountered challenges such as reduced customer visits, stringent health protocols, and supply chain issues. In the interim, there was a significant increase in the number of individuals who were making their first-time purchases online through e-commerce platforms. Among other items, the definition of "essential" was broadened to encompass work-from-home tools, indoor entertainment, and wellness products. Digital transformation, which was previously regarded as a long-term strategy, was abruptly elevated to an immediate priority. Traditional supply chains underwent rapid digital transformations, and businesses that had previously disregarded e-commerce quickly established online storefronts. The increase in online shopping during the pandemic was not merely a temporary phenomenon; it represented a substantial and enduring transformation in our lifestyles and purchasing habits.

The era of online growth and digital consumerism was already on the rise prior to 2020. However, the pandemic put that in a boost many years ahead of it is time. Therefore, this shifted the focus for digital marketers, where you need to learn from the biggest pivot so far in this century of digital consumer behavior. If you could not adapt to digital consumer behavior at the height of the pandemic, how are you going to be able to adapt in a relatively different climate?

This brings it back to the foundation statement earlier: You must have a continuous learning mindset about your consumers. At times, this learning is willing and, at times, forced. The forced part is when you must understand the emergence and deliberate *need* for consumers to change their habits because of a major event such as a pandemic. Therefore, if you are building a foundational comprehension of what digital consumer behavior is beyond definition, it is also in the sentiment of *how* you think about it beyond *what* it is.

The Intersection of Technology, Psychology, and Strategy

A Strategic Intersection

Digital consumer behavior lies at the critical intersection of technology, psychology, and strategy. Understanding how these elements converge is essential for businesses looking to thrive in today's digital landscape. Technology provides the platforms, psychology explains the motivations, and strategy aligns these insights to drive business success. This triad must be seamlessly integrated to create meaningful interactions with consumers who now expect personalized, instant, and engaging experiences online.

Technology: The Driving Force

Technology is the engine behind digital consumer behavior. It is not just about having a presence online; it's about how you leverage tools like data analytics, AI, and digital platforms to meet consumer needs. The key is in the application—how you use technology to gather insights, enhance customer experiences, and streamline operations. Businesses that excel in digital consumer engagement are those that harness technology not as an end but as a means to understand and anticipate consumer behavior.

Psychology: Understanding the Why

Psychology provides the "why" behind consumer actions. It is not enough to know what consumers are doing online; you must understand why they do it. Are they driven by convenience, influenced by social proof, or motivated by fear of missing out (FOMO)? These psychological drivers are the foundation of effective digital marketing strategies. By tapping into the psychological aspects of consumer behavior, businesses can craft messages and experiences that resonate deeply, driving engagement and loyalty.

Strategy: The Blueprint for Success

Strategy is where technology and psychology meet to form a coherent plan. It is about setting clear objectives, identifying target audiences, and designing the consumer journey. A strong digital strategy aligns technological capabilities with psychological insights to guide consumers from awareness to purchase. This requires a deep understanding of both the digital tools at your disposal and the psychological triggers that influence consumer decisions. A well-crafted strategy turns insights into action, ensuring that every touchpoint is optimized for impact.

The Synergy: A Unified Approach

The true strength of digital consumer behavior lies in the synergy between technology, psychology, and strategy. When these elements are aligned, the result is a powerful framework for engaging consumers. It is not just about using the latest tools or understanding consumer psychology; it's about how these elements work together to create a seamless, integrated experience. This synergy is the key to staying competitive in an increasingly digital world where consumer expectations are constantly evolving.

Navigating the Future

Mastering digital consumer behavior is about more than just understanding technology or psychology in isolation. It is about strategically integrating these elements to create a unified approach that drives business success. As the digital landscape continues to evolve, businesses that can navigate this intersection effectively will be the ones that thrive. The future belongs to those who can seamlessly blend technology, psychology, and strategy into a cohesive whole, delivering experiences that not only meet but also exceed consumer expectations.

Who's Doing This Well?

Nike's Approach

Technology: Nike leverages technology through its mobile apps, such as the Nike app and Nike Training Club. These apps provide personalized experiences by tracking users' fitness activities, preferences, and purchasing history. The integration of data analytics allows Nike to offer customized product recommendations and exclusive access to new releases, driving engagement and loyalty.

Psychology: Nike expertly taps into the psychology of its consumers by promoting the idea of self-improvement and achievement. The brand's "Just Do It" slogan is a powerful motivator that resonates with consumers' aspirations. Nike also utilizes social proof by showcasing user-generated content, such as customers sharing their fitness journeys on social media, which reinforces the brand's community-centric approach.

Strategy: Nike's digital strategy is deeply integrated with its broader brand strategy. The company focuses on creating a seamless omnichannel experience where online and offline interactions complement each other. For example, consumers can use the Nike app to find products, check in-store availability, and even reserve items for try-on. Nike's strategy also includes direct-to-consumer (D2C) initiatives, such as limited-edition product drops that are only available through their digital channels, creating a sense of exclusivity and urgency.

The Nike Synergy: Nike's ability to blend technology, psychology, and strategy has made it a leader in digital consumer engagement. By providing personalized experiences, tapping into consumer motivations, and creating a cohesive omnichannel strategy, Nike continues to build strong relationships with its customers and maintain its position as a top global brand.

The Digital Consumer Funnel

You hear of this concept of the marketing funnel. It's not an uncommon marketer's terminology that most don't understand in some form or fashion. However, you need to consider that there is a flare of variation when it comes to capturing it for digital consumerism and behavior. This variation is known as the digital consumer funnel. At a high level, the funnel steps will appear the same to you. The makeup of each step, though, differs slightly in the study and strategy planning within each step of the digital consumer funnel.

The concept of "digital consumer funnel" is not attributed to a single individual; rather, it has evolved over time as digital marketing practices have developed. The traditional marketing funnel, also known as the purchase funnel or sales funnel, has been around for over a century, with the earliest version being introduced by Elias St. Elmo Lewis in the late nineteenth century. His model, known as the AIDA model (Attention, Interest, Desire, Action), laid the foundation for understanding the stages consumers go through in the purchasing process. You could say this was the first glimpse of assessing consumer behavior with actionable steps and theory. However, as dynamic and as complex digital is, adaptation is key.

As marketing shifted toward digital platforms, the traditional funnel was adapted to include the specific nuances of online consumer behavior. The digital consumer funnel emerged as marketers began recognizing the unique challenges and opportunities presented by digital channels, such as social media, search engines, and e-commerce.

Understanding the Digital Consumer Funnel

The digital consumer funnel is a modern evolution of the traditional marketing funnel, reflecting the unique behaviors and expectations of today's digitally savvy consumers. Unlike the linear and predictable journey in traditional marketing, the digital consumer funnel is more dynamic and complex, requiring marketers to understand and adapt to various touchpoints across multiple channels.

Differences Between Digital and Traditional Funnels

In a traditional marketing funnel, the path from awareness to purchase is typically linear, with consumers moving step-by-step through stages like awareness, interest, desire, and action. However, the digital consumer funnel is more fluid. Consumers can jump between stages, revisit previous ones, and engage with brands through multiple channels simultaneously.

Digital consumers are informed, empowered, and expect personalized interactions. They have access to a wealth of information at their fingertips, which influences their decision-making process in real time. This behavior necessitates that digital marketers stay attuned to each phase of the funnel, understanding the distinct needs and behaviors of consumers at every stage. The following is a summary of these phases, but future chapters will dive into them more in explanation and connection to digital strategies.

Phases of the Digital Consumer Funnel

1. **Awareness**
   - **What It Is**: The Awareness phase marks the initial point of contact between the consumer and a brand. This can happen through various digital channels, such as social media, search engines, display ads, or even influencer endorsements. At this stage, the consumer becomes aware of the brand's existence, which sets the foundation for their subsequent interactions.
   - **Digital Nuance**: Awareness is not just about visibility; it is about creating a memorable first impression. Digital business allows for instantaneous global reach, meaning a brand can gain significant exposure quickly, but it also faces fierce competition for attention. Consumers are bombarded with content, so standing out requires more than just being present; it demands relevance, creativity, and consistency. Digital awareness is also highly

measurable, allowing marketers to track how many people were exposed to their content, which channels were most effective, and how these impressions translate into further engagement.

- ○ **What Marketers Need to Do**: Marketers need to craft content that is not only eye-catching but also resonant with their target audience. Consistency across platforms ensures that when consumers encounter the brand in different digital spaces, they recognize it immediately. Utilizing data analytics to optimize where and how awareness is generated can significantly enhance the effectiveness of this phase.

2. **Consideration**
   - ○ **What It Is**: The Consideration phase is where consumers actively evaluate their options. They delve deeper into the brand, exploring its products or services, comparing them with competitors, and seeking out additional information that will aid in their decision-making process.
   - ○ **Digital Nuance**: The digital environment makes it incredibly easy for consumers to research and compare brands. Within minutes, they can read reviews, watch product videos, check social media for customer experiences, and even interact with customer service via chatbots or social media platforms. This phase is also where consumers may join e-mail lists, download white papers, or engage with retargeting ads, all of which help them gather the information they need to make an informed choice.
   - ○ **What Marketers Need to Do**: Marketers must provide rich, informative content that not only highlights the benefits of their products but also addresses potential objections or questions consumers may have. This could include detailed product descriptions, FAQs, case studies, and testimonials. Additionally, leveraging retargeting strategies can help keep the brand at the top of their mind as consumers weigh their options.

3. **Conversion**
   - ○ **What It Is**: Conversion is the critical phase where the consumer makes the decision to purchase or engage with the brand in a meaningful way, such as signing up for a service or making a purchase.

- **Digital Nuance:** In the digital space, the conversion process is often streamlined and can happen rapidly. However, it is also the phase where consumers are most likely to abandon the process if they encounter friction. Factors such as complexity of the checkout process, availability of preferred payment methods, and mobile-friendliness of the website can significantly impact conversion rates.
- **What Marketers Need to Do:** To optimize conversions, marketers should focus on reducing any potential barriers that could disrupt the purchasing process. This includes simplifying the checkout process, offering a variety of payment options, and ensuring that the website is optimized for mobile devices. Additionally, clear, and compelling calls-to-action (CTA) are essential to guide consumers toward making a decision. Providing real-time customer support, such as live chat, helps address last-minute concerns that might otherwise prevent a conversion.

4. **Loyalty**
   - **What It Is:** Once a consumer has made a purchase, the focus shifts to building a long-term relationship, fostering loyalty, and encouraging repeat business.
   - **Digital Nuance:** Loyalty in the digital age is heavily influenced by ongoing engagement and personalized experiences. Digital channels offer numerous opportunities to maintain contact with customers, from e-mail marketing and social media interactions to personalized offers and loyalty programs. Brands can use data collected during the consumer's journey to tailor their communications and offers, making them more relevant and appealing.
   - **What Marketers Need to Do:** Marketers should implement strategies that reinforce the brand's value and maintain a positive relationship with customers. Loyalty programs, personalized e-mail campaigns, and consistent engagement through social media are all effective tools. Moreover, responding promptly to customer feedback and continuously offering value, whether through content, exclusive deals, or superior customer service, can help turn one-time buyers into repeat customers.

5. **Advocacy**
   1. **What It Is**: Advocacy is the goal of the consumer funnel, where satisfied customers become vocal supporters of the brand, actively promoting it to others through word-of-mouth, social media, or online reviews.
   2. **Digital Nuance**: The digital world amplifies advocacy, allowing customer endorsements to reach a wide audience quickly. Social media platforms, review sites, and even personal blogs can serve as powerful channels for customer advocacy. In this phase, the brand's online reputation becomes critical, as potential customers often rely heavily on the opinions and experiences of others when making decisions.
   3. **What Marketers Need to Do**: To encourage advocacy, marketers should focus on creating exceptional customer experiences that inspire customers to share their positive experiences with others. This can be facilitated by encouraging user-generated content, offering incentives for referrals, and actively engaging with customers who share their experiences online. Additionally, managing and responding to online reviews, whether positive or negative, is crucial in shaping the brand's reputation and encouraging advocacy.

The digital consumer funnel reflects a more complex and interconnected journey. Marketers must be agile, data-driven, and customer-centric, ensuring that they meet the consumer at every touchpoint with relevant and engaging content.

It is Circular, Not Linear

The digital consumer funnel is not a linear process; it is a circular journey that reflects the ongoing relationship between your brand and your customers. Unlike traditional models where the consumer's journey ends with a purchase, the digital funnel recognizes that consumers continuously interact with brands well after their initial purchase. As a business professional, you must understand that each interaction—whether it is a follow-up e-mail or a social media engagement or a new product offering—can reopen the possibility of further engagement, retention,

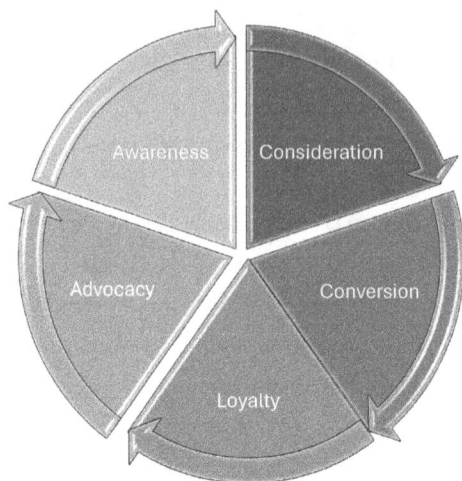

Figure 1.1 Circular digital consumer funnel

and advocacy. The circular nature of this funnel is driven by consumers' constant access to information and their expectation of a seamless, personalized experience across all touchpoints (Figure 1.1).

Over time, with experience, you begin to acknowledge the circularity of the digital consumer funnel is essential. You cannot just focus on one-time conversions; your strategy must aim at building long-term relationships. Each phase of the funnel, from awareness to advocacy, is interconnected. You must deliver value at any stage to avoid disengagement and lost opportunities. That is why it's critical to create a cohesive, omnichannel experience that not only guides consumers through their initial journey but also keeps them coming back into the funnel. By doing so, you foster loyalty and drive sustained growth through continuous consumer engagement. Further strategies, applications, and insights will be covered throughout this book.

Key Points

- Digital consumer behavior is continuous learning rather than just knowing.
- The intersection of psychology, technology, and strategy is the core component of digital consumer behavior.
- The digital consumer funnel is unique, unlike traditional marketing funnels.

As We Move Ahead

Building your psyche on the foundation of digital consumer behavior allows you to have that foundation in mind as you proceed down the path of exploring each phase of the funnel further. You will be able to ideate clearly how to assess, analyze, learn, and implement strategies through the continuous learning process. However, you cannot do it alone. The entire entity of your organization needs to understand this, believe it, come together, and incorporate it into the overall strategy. The next chapter explores the ways in which we can be stewards of change by adopting this mindset and integrating it into the DNA of the company.

CHAPTER 2

Fostering an Organizational Culture of Digital Consumer Centricity

To win in the marketplace, you must first win in the workplace.
—Doug Conant

Chapter Overview

More is needed to understand digital consumer behavior on an individual level. Organizations must also undergo a cultural shift to embrace and integrate digital consumer behavior theory and strategy into their core values and operations. This chapter explores how businesses can cultivate a culture that places the digital consumer at the center of decision-making, driving success in today's digitally driven marketplace.

What Kind of Party Are You Having?

You like a good party, right? At least some gathering where you feel you belong and engaged in something of interest. Consumers want the same thing: a party they are invited to and where they feel they belong, fit in, and enjoy their interests. However, before you invite your consumers to that party, ask yourself—are the hosts on the same page on building and conducting that party? Are there mixed views on the entertainment, refreshments, and overall reasons for having the party? If there is, the party wouldn't be as fun or as engaging, would it? Also, some guests would decide to leave early or even not show up.

Jeff Bezos once said, "We see our customers as guests to a party, and we are the hosts. It's our job every day to make every important aspect of the customer experience a little bit better."

If you think of your digital marketing as a party, there might be an outlet for more creative thinking, innovation, and fun among the hosts. The more aligned the hosts, the more cohesive the party plan, execution, and value to the guests. No one wants to go to that party where the decorations are messy. No one wants to go to a party where the entertainment is annoying or confusing. Lastly, no one wants to go to a party that misses the mark on their initial interest or intent. Therefore, it takes the party committee, hosts, and all associated partners to join in an alliance to ensure the party is the best it can be.

The Hard Truth

In reality, many companies think they are consumer-centric but are not. At least partly or at some minimal level. Most companies in the 2020s believe in the importance of being customer-centric. However, their capability to integrate it into their DNA of digital strategy still has opportunities for improvement. In their report, "The Disconnected Customer" (2017), Capgemini noted that businesses and customers are "miles apart on the customer experience." They found that 75 percent of companies believe they are customer-centric, while only 30 percent of customers agree. This notes the gap in company belief versus consumer perception. It's that significant gap that puts the need for digital marketers to start becoming stewards in the organization for a cultural shift in not just becoming consumer-centric but also digitally focused on this principle. At first thought, I knew it seemed daunting, complex, and challenging to be the steward. But, remember, one cannot do it alone to be competitive. It is not just the digital marketing team that can deliver either. It truly takes a village to transform the company culture. Let's take a look at how this is done.

The Core of Digital Consumer Centricity

To build a customer-centric culture, everyone within the organization must prioritize the customer in every aspect of their work. This means considering the customer's needs, feelings, and challenges, whether you are directly interacting with them or working behind the scenes.

A customer-centric culture is not a philosophy for an organization; it is a principle. Perhaps it is a mandate of standard best practice to ensure validity in some executives' minds. This involves continuously asking how any action will impact the customer, what value it will deliver, and how it will address their needs or solve their problems.

The concept is simple. It focuses on the fact that customers' needs, preferences, and perspectives are not just considered but are deeply integrated into the very core of the organization. This means the customer is at the heart of every company decision, conversation, and action. It is about ensuring that every process, strategy, and interaction is designed with the customer in mind, aiming to create value and deliver a seamless, positive experience at every touchpoint.

In such a culture, every department, from product development to marketing to customer service, collaborates to understand and meet customer needs. The customer's voice is heard and valued in all aspects of the business, influencing everything from product design to service delivery. This approach goes beyond satisfying the customer; it's about anticipating their needs and exceeding their expectations. By embedding the customer at the center of the organization's fabric, businesses can build stronger relationships, foster loyalty, and differentiate themselves in a competitive market. Creating a customer-centric culture requires a commitment from leadership, buy-in from every team member, and the ability to adapt and evolve based on customer feedback and changing market conditions. Ultimately, it's about recognizing that the customer is the driving force behind the company's success, and every action should reflect this understanding.

It's focused on solid leadership as well. Cuddy et al. (2013) from *Harvard Business Review* state—"When we judge others—especially our leaders—we look first at two characteristics: how lovable they are (their warmth, communion, or trustworthiness) and how fearsome they are (their strength, agency, or competence)." This is that type of culture–environment connection needed in an environment of customer-centric culture, where leaders can be judged upon an atmosphere of lovability and fearsomeness. How can we outwardly connect with consumers if inwardly we don't have more lovability in leadership to embrace customer centricity versus a fear of it?

The layer within digital business adds more complexity for companies to become truly digital consumer centric. The abundance of technological advances at a rapid pace, fused with continuous changes in the behaviors of online consumers, truly enhances the backbone and foundation of culture a company needs to have to compete. As stated before, digital consumer behavior is dynamic, circular, and constantly changing. However, the framework to remain consumer-centric through that volatility should stay consistent and foundational.

Theory to Practice

Theory. When I say that word, do you cringe? Yes, we must acknowledge they exist. It brings us back to those business classes or PBS specials we'd watch to learn about a prominent figure in academics and their thought process on something grand at scale. They may be forced to memorize the pillars, framework, or methods.

Why are theories developed in the first place? I believe in business; they hold a lot of weight, from when they were developed to how we apply them today. Yes, it may seem as if we are bridging academics and industry here, but isn't that the point? As both a professor and experienced executive, this is the first gap I have seen when it comes to knowledge management in the workplace, especially in digital marketing. There is an opportunity to advance some of these consumer behavior theories into actual application.

It can be the generation starter to building that unique company culture that is needed to become more consumer-centric. Understanding company culture theories is not just about grasping abstract concepts— it's about applying these frameworks to the practical challenges of modern business, particularly in creating a consumer-centric organization. Let's explore how each of these prominent company culture theories can be leveraged to enhance digital consumer behavior centricity within organizations.

Edgar Schein's Organizational Culture Model (1980s)

Edgar Schein's Organizational Culture Model, developed in the 1980s, divides organizational culture into three levels: artifacts, espoused values, and basic underlying assumptions. Artifacts are the visible and tangible elements of culture, such as dress code, office layout, and formal processes. Espoused values are the stated norms and philosophies, like a company's mission statement or code of ethics. The deepest level, basic underlying assumptions, consists of unconscious, taken-for-granted beliefs that truly define the essence of the organization's culture (Figure 2.1).

Connection to Digital Consumer Centricity

To be consumer-centric in the digital age, a company's underlying assumptions must prioritize the customer, driving decisions that enhance user experience across digital platforms. Misalignment between these levels—such as outdated technology conflicting with a stated focus on customer satisfaction—can erode trust and consistency in consumer experiences. Schein's model underscores the importance of aligning all cultural levels to build a reliable, consumer-focused organization.

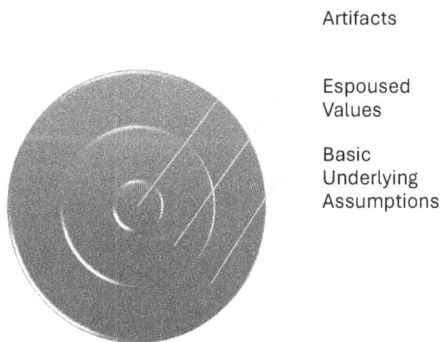

Artifacts

Espoused Values

Basic Underlying Assumptions

Figure 2.1 Edgar Schein's Organizational Culture Model

Who Has Done It? Spotify

Spotify's core belief that music should be accessible and personalized to every listener drives its operations at all cultural levels. At the artifact level, this belief manifests in features like Discover Weekly and personalized playlists. Their espoused value of "putting users first" is reflected in continuous improvements to the user interface and music recommendation algorithms. This alignment ensures that Spotify delivers a consistent and engaging consumer experience, making it a leader in digital music streaming.

Charles Handy's Four Types of Culture (1976)

Charles Handy proposed his model in 1976, categorizing organizational culture into four types: Power Culture, Role Culture, Task Culture, and Person Culture. Each of these cultures has different implications for how an organization operates and interacts with its employees and customers (Figure 2.2).

- **Power Culture:** Centralized control, where decisions are made by a few individuals.
- **Role Culture:** Bureaucratic, with clearly defined roles and responsibilities.
- **Task Culture:** Team-oriented, focused on getting specific jobs done.
- **Person Culture:** Individual-focused, where the organization exists to serve the individuals within it.

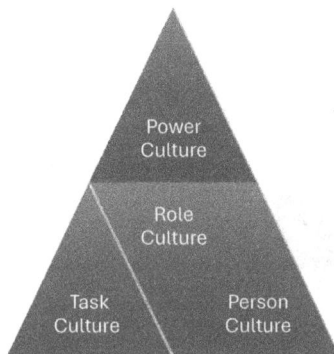

Figure 2.2 Charles Handy's four types of culture

Connection to Digital Consumer Centricity

- **Power Culture** might hinder consumer focus if too centralized, but strong leadership can drive quick consumer-centric decisions.
- **Role Culture** may struggle with fast digital changes, but clear roles can maintain service consistency.
- **Task Culture** promotes flexibility, which is ideal for adapting to consumer needs.
- **Person Culture** fosters creativity in addressing consumer demands but needs alignment with broader strategies to avoid inconsistency.

Who Has Done It? Netflix (Task Culture)

Netflix thrives on a task culture where teams are empowered to make decisions and innovate rapidly. This flexibility is key to their ability to adapt to changes in viewer preferences and technology quickly. By focusing on data-driven insights and consumer behavior, Netflix teams can quickly introduce new features like personalized recommendations, interactive content, and original programming. This alignment with task culture ensures that Netflix remains agile and consumer-focused in the highly competitive streaming industry.

Gert Hofstede's Cultural Dimensions Theory (1960s)

Gert Hofstede's Cultural Dimensions Theory, developed in the late 1960s, initially aimed to analyze national cultures but has been widely applied to organizational culture as well. The theory identifies six dimensions that influence culture: Power Distance, Individualism versus Collectivism, Masculinity versus Femininity, Uncertainty Avoidance, Long-term versus Short-term Orientation, and Indulgence versus Restraint (Figure 2.3).

Connection to Digital Consumer Centricity

These dimensions help organizations understand how internal culture affects their ability to meet consumer needs. For example, low power distance enables quicker consumer feedback loops, while a long-term

Power Distance	Individualism vs Collectivism	Masculinity vs Femininity
Uncertainty Avoidance	Long-Term vs. Short-Term Avoidance	Short-term vs Long-term Orientation
	Indulgence vs Restraint	

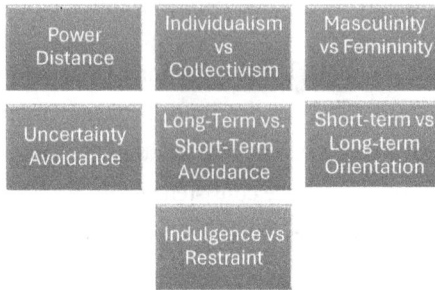

Figure 2.3 Gert Hofstede's Cultural Dimensions Theory (1960s)

orientation fosters sustainable customer relationships. Analyzing these factors allows companies to adapt and optimize their practices for better consumer engagement in the digital marketplace.

Who Has Done It? Airbnb (Individualism vs. Collectivism and Low Power Distance)

Airbnb operates with a blend of individualism and collectivism, empowering hosts (individualism) to personalize their offerings while fostering a sense of community among users (collectivism). Their low-power-distance culture encourages open communication, enabling them to rapidly implement changes based on host and guest feedback. This cultural alignment allows Airbnb to continuously innovate and improve its platform, ensuring that it meets the diverse needs of its global user base and enhances consumer centricity in the digital marketplace.

Importance for Business Practitioners

For modern business practitioners, understanding these cultural theories is essential in creating an organization that is truly consumer-centric, particularly in the digital age. The theories offer frameworks to diagnose and address cultural misalignments that impede the organization's ability to respond effectively to consumer needs. By leveraging insights from Schein, Handy, and Hofstede, practitioners can cultivate a culture that supports agility, innovation, and a deep commitment to consumer satisfaction—key elements in maintaining a competitive edge in today's fast-paced digital marketplace.

Ultimately, the alignment of company culture with digital consumer centricity is not just a matter of internal coherence; it's a strategic necessity that can significantly enhance a company's ability to attract, retain, and delight customers in the digital era.

The Roots of Change

The easiest analogy is that your roots as a business are your foundation. Are your roots weak? Is your tree able to stand against the climate, wind, or storm? Is your tree able to grow amidst the growing trees around them? Can your tree even stand out in the forest? If you cannot answer any of those questions in a positive manner, then you need to stop worrying about cleaning up the leaves that have fallen or the bark of the tree that needs to be cleaned up. It's time to go back to the underground and inspect those roots. This is where you, as the cultivator of digital stewardship, step in and begin the transformation.

It starts with *authentic* core values. Remember, core values should be part of your company's DNA, like the cells of your body. This is where realness and authenticity step in. Mission and vision statements are aspirations, but core values are the daily practices conducted by a company to work toward those aspirations. Therefore, if a company aspires to be the top brand in its respective digital marketplace, there must be an integration of a consumer-centric value system. To generate customer centricity as part of a company's core value system, a comprehensive approach is required, encompassing strategic alignment, cultural transformation, communication planning, and change management.

Strategic Alignment

From my early years as a marketing analyst to the rank of Chief Revenue Officer, the consistent gap I found in some of the organizations I worked for was a lack of truly living the core values we preached. No matter the level of the position, it was a keen observation. No one internally wants to admit it when we are not practicing what we preach. Unless it is acknowledged and affirmed that improvement is needed, the rest of the notion of becoming more than what we are is not going to happen. It's as simple as that.

Now, it does not necessarily mean the phrase "customer-centric" needs to be in the list of values you publish on the "About Us" page of your website. Rather, it can be a choice of related text, content, phraseology, and key terms and descriptors that fit the best tone of your brand. Branding is still important here. However, a further implication is that, to our digital consumers, the branding component in core values is more about what is displayed and our action versus what is written.

First, get everyone, and that means everyone is on the same page. Generally, it must start with leadership and cascade. No matter the structure of the company, the culture still comes from a place of role-modeling. The motivation, decision-making, planning, and execution generally stem from some leadership entity. Now, inspiration does not have to start with leadership. The departments or teams that start the advocation can spark the interest of leaders to listen and understand.

Being a Digital Consumer Champion

What It Means to Be One

A digital consumer champion is an advocate within a company who ensures that the needs and experiences of digital consumers are central to every strategic decision and operational process. This role goes beyond understanding digital tools—it requires deep empathy for the consumer's journey and a commitment to continuously adapting the company's offerings to meet their evolving needs. The digital consumer champion acts as a bridge between leadership, operational teams, and consumers, ensuring that all initiatives align with enhancing the digital customer experience.

How to Be One

To be an effective digital consumer champion, you must develop a profound understanding of consumer behavior through constant engagement with data and feedback. It's crucial to advocate for consumer-centric decisions in every strategic discussion, ensuring that the consumer's perspective is always considered.

Leading by example is vital; demonstrating a commitment to consumer satisfaction in daily actions reinforces this focus across the organization. Building strong cross-functional relationships is also essential, as it ensures that all departments work toward common consumer-centric goals. Finally, measuring and sharing the successes of these initiatives help reinforce the value of a consumer-first approach and encourages its broader adoption within the company.

How to Influence

Influencing others as a digital consumer champion involves educating and inspiring colleagues about the importance of consumer centricity. This can be achieved by sharing insights and success stories that illustrate the positive impact of a consumer-focused strategy. Creating a shared vision of a consumer-centric organization is also critical, as it aligns the entire company with common goals.

Building a network of likeminded champions within the organization helps amplify the consumer's voice and fosters a culture of collaboration. Additionally, leveraging data to support your arguments is key to driving change and ensuring that consumer centricity remains a top priority. Encouraging a consumer-first culture through training, recognition, and embedding consumer-centric metrics into performance reviews will help solidify this approach as a core aspect of the company's values.

Setting the Arena

Once the troops are rallied through advocation, it's important to establish the arena where this alignment can flourish next. It's time to ask some tough questions in order to do this. Some of these are uncomfortable but necessary:

- Do you have any silos? Really, are there ANY?
- Does everyone, from the field employee to the board of directors, understand what digital consumer behavior and centricity is?
- What are the communication barriers? Why do they exist? How do we attack them?

Sound familiar? Yes, it's internal analysis time. However, with the realness of evaluation, it is possible to get to the core of the company culture. Really digging to the roots and either enhancing a well-established foundation or repotting the soil to ensure change and new growth.

It's necessary through this exercise, while perhaps not glamorous or fan-favorite internally. It is this internal assessment that has given me a firsthand glimpse into the faults of some organizations in their efforts to transform themselves, not just digitally but even with their market dynamics. If you had the time and money to renovate your home to get it more up-to-date for yourself, your neighborhood, and guests and enhance its value, then why wouldn't you do that for your company? Renovation is not giving up or necessarily always starting over. It's augmenting what has already been successful in the connection with consumers and just modernizing the company in order to be able to compete and thrive.

To successfully assimilate and integrate digital consumer champions into your organization, it's essential to create a working environment that fosters collaboration, aligns goals, and supports the continuous development of consumer-centric strategies. This environment must be conducive to open communication, cross-functional teamwork, and a shared commitment to putting the consumer at the heart of all decisions.

Cultivate a Collaborative Culture

Start by fostering a culture of collaboration where digital consumer champions are encouraged to work closely with all departments, from marketing to product development to customer service. This cross-functional approach ensures that consumer insights are seamlessly integrated into every aspect of the business. Regular team meetings, joint workshops, and shared project goals can help break down silos and promote a unified focus on consumer-centric strategies.

Align on Clear, Consumer-Centric Objectives

Ensure that all teams within the organization are aligned on clear, consumer-centric objectives. This involves setting measurable goals that reflect the company's commitment to consumer satisfaction, such as improving customer retention rates, enhancing user experience, or increasing customer engagement. Digital consumer champions should be involved in the strategic planning process to ensure these objectives are understood and prioritized across the organization.

Provide the Necessary Tools and Resources

Equip digital consumer champions with the tools and resources they need to succeed. This includes access to advanced analytics platforms, customer feedback systems, and Customer Relationship Management (CRM) tools that enable them to gather, analyze, and act on consumer data effectively. Additionally, providing ongoing training and professional development opportunities helps ensure that these champions stay ahead of trends and best practices in consumer behavior.

Establish Open Communication Channels

Create open communication channels that allow digital consumer champions to share insights and collaborate with other team members regularly. This could be facilitated through digital platforms like Slack or Microsoft Teams, as well as through more formalized channels such as regular strategy meetings or town halls. Encouraging transparency and the free flow of information helps ensure that consumer insights are consistently incorporated into strategic decisions.

Foster a Supportive Leadership Structure

Leadership plays a crucial role in integrating digital consumer champions. Leaders should actively support and endorse the role of these champions, ensuring they have a voice at the highest levels of decision-making. By publicly recognizing and rewarding consumer-centric achievements, leaders can reinforce the importance of this focus and encourage others to align with these values.

Promote Continuous Feedback and Improvement

Finally, the working environment should promote a culture of continuous feedback and improvement. Encourage digital consumer champions to seek feedback from both consumers and colleagues regularly and to use this input to refine strategies and practices. This iterative approach helps keep the organization agile and responsive to changing consumer needs, ensuring that the company remains competitive in the digital marketplace.

By building an environment that emphasizes collaboration, alignment, and continuous improvement, organizations can effectively integrate digital consumer champions into their teams. This ensures that the company's strategies are consistently aligned with the evolving needs of its customers, driving sustained success in their respective industries.

Beyond Digital Transformation

Digital transformation—it's the buzzword that's been echoing through the halls of businesses for over two decades. Companies have been, are, and will continue to be on this journey of transformation for years to come. But let's be clear: Digital transformation is not just about adopting the latest technology or moving your operations to the cloud. It's far more profound. When it comes to integrating digital consumer centricity, this transformation goes beyond mere technology upgrades; it's about embedding consumer-centric thinking into the very DNA of your company.

Omol (2023) conducted a study focused on customer centricity at the core of digital transformation. The study stresses that organizations must prioritize customer-centric strategies as the backbone of their digital transformation efforts. This involves a shift in focus from just automating processes or cutting costs to using data-driven insights to deeply understand customer needs and preferences. By doing so, companies can ensure that every interaction is personalized, relevant, and valuable to the customer. This approach not only improves customer satisfaction but also builds long-term loyalty, which is essential in today's competitive landscape.

Moreover, the ethical use of AI and data is highlighted as a critical component. Companies are encouraged to adopt AI solutions that are transparent, fair, and aligned with societal values. This ensures that the deployment of these technologies enhances the customer experience by providing personalized and meaningful interactions rather than alienating customers through impersonal or invasive practices. Ultimately, the focus is that the success of digital transformation efforts depends on how well companies integrate customer-centric principles into their use of technology.

More Than Technology Adoption

Sure, technology adoption is a critical piece of the puzzle, but it's only the beginning. Simply investing in new software or upgrading your IT infrastructure won't automatically make your company more consumer-centric. Technology must be wielded with purpose and guided by a deep understanding of consumer needs. It's not just about having the latest tools; it's about using those tools to create meaningful, personalized experiences for your customers. This means that your digital platforms, data analytics, and customer interfaces must all be strategically aligned to serve your consumer-centric goals.

Building True Partnerships

Digital consumer centricity also requires forming strong partnerships—both internal and external. Internally, this means ensuring that all departments, from marketing to IT to customer service, are working together seamlessly toward the common goal of enhancing the customer experience. Externally, it means choosing technology and software providers who understand and share your commitment to consumer centricity. Your partners should be more than just vendors; they should be invested collaborators who are as committed to your consumer-driven mission as you are. This alignment ensures that every technological investment is directly contributing to a more consumer-focused operation.

Involving External Stakeholders

But the transformation doesn't stop within the walls of your organization. True digital consumer centricity demands that your external stakeholders—suppliers, distributors, and even customers themselves—are part of the process. They need to be engaged and invested in the evolution of your consumer-centric strategies. This might involve co-creating products with key customers, integrating suppliers into your digital platforms, or working closely with distributors to ensure that your consumer experience is consistent across all touchpoints. Every stakeholder must be aligned with your vision of consumer centricity, creating a cohesive and unified effort that extends beyond the company itself.

Embedding Consumer Centricity into Your DNA

Let's be bold here: If you think digital transformation is just a checkbox exercise or a one-time project, you're missing the point entirely. This is about a fundamental shift in how your company operates. It's about making consumer centricity the core of your business strategy and ensuring that every aspect of your digital transformation supports this goal. The companies that will thrive in the future are those that go beyond superficial changes and make a deep, systemic commitment to putting the customer at the center of everything they do.

So, Ready to Party?

Companies that fail to embrace this comprehensive approach to digital transformation will find themselves left behind. The future belongs to those who not only adopt the latest technology but also align their entire ecosystem—internal teams, technology partners, and external stakeholders—around a shared commitment to digital consumer centricity. This isn't just about keeping up with the times; it's about leading the charge and setting the standard for what it means to be truly consumer-centric digitally.

Now, let's go back to that focus of planning that party. Are all the hosts on the same page? Do the entertainment, decorations, and themes all make sense? Do we have the right guests on the guest list? If we can now say yes to all of the above with true certainty, then it's time to party!

Key Points

- Alignment among all stakeholders is essential for executing a cohesive consumer-centric strategy.
- Consumer-centric culture requires more than good intentions; it necessitates a comprehensive cultural shift within the organization.
- Achieving true digital consumer centricity is an ongoing process that must be integrated into the company's DNA through strategic alignment and continuous adaptation.

As We Move Ahead

Ultimately, digital transformation and integrating consumer centricity are not just an initiative; they are a revolution. They require a bold, integrated approach where technology adoption, strategic partnerships, and stakeholder involvement all converge to create a company that lives and breathes consumer centricity. This is the future of business, and it's happening now. Are you ready to lead the way? If so, the next chapter starts at the top of the digital consumer funnel, focusing on awareness and generating that thing we call "a buzz."

CHAPTER 3

Digital Discovery and Awareness

It's not about having the right opportunities. It's about handling the opportunities right.

—Mark Hunter

Chapter Overview

Are you out there? Is anyone home? We must remember that the best-looking, engaging, and enticing website, mobile app, or even physical location is no good if it cannot be found. You have this "thing" you want to sell, service, or provide, right? Well, online, so does everyone else. This chapter speaks to the foundations of consumer awareness at the driver's seat of digital strategy. Moreover, it provides a shift in organizational thinking as well, that you need to invest in the consumer's discovery process to avoid investing in anything else.

Best Prices and Products Are Not Always Enough

Didn't someone once say what is here today could quickly be gone tomorrow? I've heard that. In fact, it's a phrase that often haunted me during a time of crisis when a former retailer I worked for was struggling to remain in business. Actually, they did go out of brick-and-mortar and business-to-consumer (B2C) e-commerce business but remained business-to-business (B2B), at least for now. A key reason was that the retailer offered customers competitive prices and top-tier brand products. They knew their regional market well. In fact, they even had decent advertising. However, the competition in the space was fierce. As a regional retailer, it was challenging for this company to compete at a scale against national retailers. As I worked there as a middle-level merchant, I knew that the challenge was different from the products, services, or prices. It was all about relevance and just the need to be found by new and former consumers.

Despite decent regional advertising and a strong understanding of their market, the retailer ultimately needed help to keep up. The challenge wasn't with the products, services, or prices—they excelled in those areas. The real issue was staying relevant and being easily discoverable by both new and existing consumers. The senior executives believed that aggressive markdowns, frequent discounts, and relentless advertising to existing customers would suffice. Unfortunately, this approach led to razor-thin profit margins and failed to attract new consumers, sealing the company's fate.

This was the struggle I had, as we can call it, as a mid-level manager. Top-down management had their way of conducting business, and, in my mind, a more holistic thought on consumer discovery. At that level, it can be a challenge to cultivate a different mindset for the entire company, it's not a one-person show to do so. Hence, here are the tactics and reasoning for Chapter 2 that you just read.

As a mid-level manager, I recognized the importance of being found by consumers during their discovery phase. This experience taught me a valuable lesson: the need to balance consumer acquisition with retention. In every digital strategy I've led since, I've emphasized the importance of driving traffic to both e-commerce sites and brick-and-mortar stores while nurturing long-term relationships with loyal customers. This balance doesn't always require a 50/50 split, but neglecting either aspect at any point is a recipe for mismanaging your digital business.

Digital Consumers Are Always Setting Sail

Consumers are constantly on the move, exploring new options and seeking new experiences or products. It is implicit that consumer behavior is dynamic and ever-changing, much like sailors who are always embarking on new voyages. Brands need to continuously adapt and innovate to keep up with consumers' evolving preferences and desires.

These insights align with recent market research, which underscores the fluidity of consumer behavior and the necessity of adapting to maintain visibility. For instance, 24 percent of global consumers are increasingly shopping across multiple channels, demonstrating the importance of being present and discoverable wherever consumers may search (NIQ,

"Consumer Outlook 2024"). Furthermore, while 66 percent of consumers actively seek out deals, the challenge remains for businesses to ensure they are visible during this crucial discovery period (Intelligence Node 2024). Without this visibility, even the most competitive prices and premium products can fail to resonate with potential customers.

The beauty of digital marketing versus traditional is that you have more robust capabilities to be at the right time and the right place for those discovery moments with potential consumers. Leveraging data, analytics, and innovative automated marketing tech stacks, it's not that the tools don't exist; it's the need to get out of your comfort zone at times. The sense of comfort that you have "enough" web traffic or digital consumer count is a danger to growth and sustainability. You should celebrate the success of top customer counts and ongoing trends of sustained loyalty. You should not, though, use the celebration as a weakness to ignore or forget the changing power of consumers and their ability to be attracted elsewhere.

Awareness: The Gateway to Engagement

The awareness step of the digital consumer funnel is the initial stage where potential consumers first encounter your brand, product, or service. This phase is critical because it sets the foundation for the entire consumer journey and is where your relationship with potential consumers begins.

Your primary objective during this stage is to capture their attention, ensuring that your brand becomes visible in an increasingly competitive digital landscape. Whether through search engine optimization (SEO), social media marketing, content marketing, or paid advertisements, creating awareness is about making sure that your brand stands out from the crowd and becomes the choice they remember.

As someone responsible for guiding the digital strategy, understanding the significance of the awareness step is crucial. This phase is when potential consumers decide whether to engage further with your brand or move on to others. Effective awareness strategies increase the likelihood that consumers will progress through the funnel to consideration and purchase. However, this stage is not just about getting noticed; it's about making a lasting impression. A brand that successfully captures attention during this stage lays the groundwork for deeper consumer engagement and long-term loyalty, which is the goal of any marketing effort.

Online First Impressions Always Matter

The handshake, eye contact, well-spoken, and friendly in-person first impression matter in business. It's also on a very 1:1 basis, usually unless a speaker is at some conference speaking to a bunch of potential consumers or clients.

However, in digital, the first impression is more volatile. There is a constant set of first impressions happening at the same time in many different potential avenues, with a wide variety of potential outlets. In my mind, it is a first impression set of force multipliers that we have to manage in digital marketing. A multi-prong approach usually is down to a singular 1:1 engagement. What does that mean? This means that our digital marketing is widespread, reaching many, but we are really only trying to distill it down to a tangible 1:1 impression with a consumer to seek their potential interest in us.

Research indicates that we have as little as **7 seconds** to make a lasting first impression that sparks initial interest. Online, it can be even shorter. Google states that in these fleeting moments, your brand's digital presence must communicate value, credibility, and relevance.

For business executives, this means that every element of your digital strategy—from website design to content delivery—must be meticulously crafted to engage and resonate with your audience immediately. A solid first impression can set the tone for the entire customer journey, influencing perceptions and decisions long before a deeper interaction occurs.

In a world where consumers are bombarded with options, failing to capture attention swiftly could mean losing out to competitors who have mastered the art of making those critical first seconds count. Investing in a well-optimized, visually appealing, and user-centric digital experience is not just a marketing consideration; it's a business imperative that directly impacts your brand's ability to attract and retain customers in the digital age.

Digital Presence Audit

Have you conducted your digital presence audit lately? Have you ever done one? A digital presence audit is a comprehensive evaluation of all the touchpoints where your brand interacts with customers in the digital space. It involves assessing your website, social media profiles, online advertising efforts, content marketing strategies, and any other digital assets to understand how effectively your brand is being represented online. The audit provides a clear picture of your current digital footprint, identifying strengths, weaknesses, opportunities, and threats that can impact your brand's ability to attract and engage potential customers.

Why Is a Digital Presence Audit Important?

Before diving into new acquisition strategies, it is crucial to understand where your brand currently stands in the digital landscape. A digital presence audit serves as a diagnostic tool that helps you (Figure 3.1):

Key Areas	Description
Identify Gaps and Opportunities	By thoroughly assessing your digital presence, you can uncover areas where your brand may be underperforming or lacking visibility. This insight allows you to address weaknesses and capitalize on missed opportunities.
Ensure Consistency	Consistency across all digital channels is critical to building a solid brand identity. An audit helps you ensure that your messaging, visual elements, and tone are aligned across platforms, providing a cohesive experience for your audience.
Benchmark Performance	Understanding your current performance metrics, such as website traffic, social media engagement, and conversion rates, allows you to set realistic goals and measure the effectiveness of future strategies.
Improve Customer Experience	By evaluating how users interact with your brand online, you can identify areas for improvement in user experience, leading to higher engagement and satisfaction.
Enhance Strategic Planning	With a clear understanding of your digital presence, you can make informed decisions about where to allocate resources, which channels to prioritize, and what strategies to implement to maximize your brand's reach and impact.

Figure 3.1 Digital presence assessment key areas

A Step-by-Step Guide

A digital presence audit is not just a diagnostic tool; it's a strategic necessity that lays the foundation for informed decision-making and sustainable growth. This audit provides a holistic view of your digital footprint, enabling you to optimize performance, enhance visibility, and drive meaningful engagement. Below is an expert-led, detailed framework to guide you through conducting an effective digital presence audit (Figure 3.2).

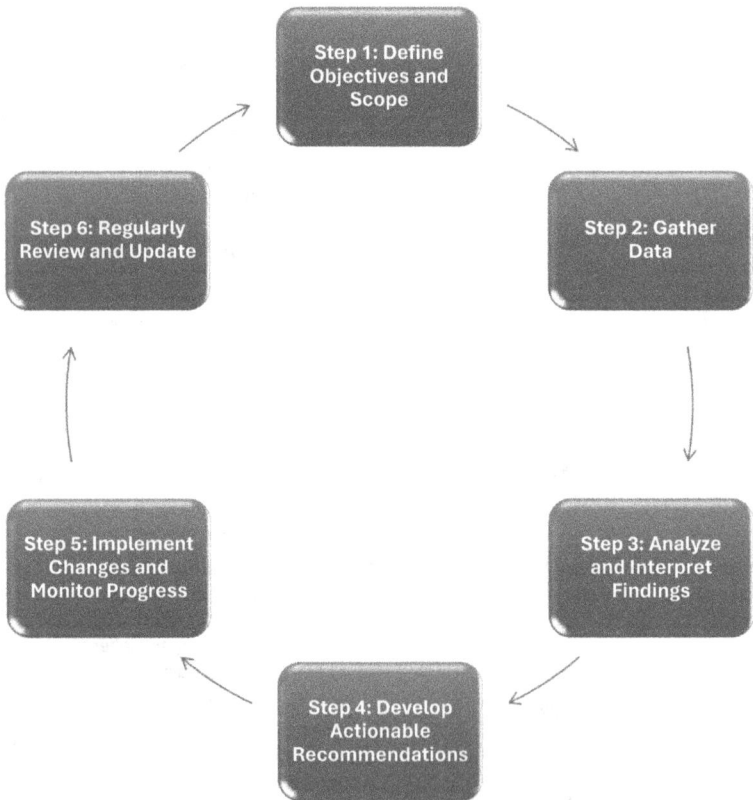

Step 1: Define Objectives and Scope

Step 2: Gather Data

Step 3: Analyze and Interpret Findings

Step 4: Develop Actionable Recommendations

Step 5: Implement Changes and Monitor Progress

Step 6: Regularly Review and Update

Figure 3.2 Digital presence audit step-by-step guide

Step 1: Define Objectives and Scope

Set Clear, Measurable Goals: The first and most crucial step in a digital presence audit is to establish clear, measurable objectives. This involves asking strategic questions: What are you aiming to achieve with this audit? Are you looking to increase brand visibility, drive more traffic to your website, enhance user experience, or improve conversion rates? Perhaps you're interested in understanding how your digital assets are performing compared to those of your competitors. By clearly defining your goals, you can focus your audit on the areas that will have the most significant impact on your business.

Consider setting SMART (Specific, Measurable, Achievable, Relevant, Time-bound) objectives. For example, instead of broadly aiming to "increase website traffic," set a goal to "increase organic website traffic by 25 percent within six months." This specificity will guide your audit process and provide a clear benchmark for success.

Determine the Scope of Your Audit: Once your objectives are set, it's essential to determine the scope of your audit. A digital presence audit can be broad, covering multiple aspects of your online presence, or it can be more focused, depending on your goals. Key areas to consider include:

- **Website Performance:** Evaluate the technical and content aspects of your website.
- **Social Media Profiles:** Assess engagement, consistency, and brand alignment across platforms.
- **Content Marketing:** Analyze the effectiveness of your content strategy in engaging and converting your audience.
- **Online Advertising:** Review the performance and return on investment (ROI) of your digital ad campaigns.
- **Competitor Analysis:** Compare your digital presence to that of your key competitors to identify opportunities and threats.

By defining the scope, you ensure that your audit is comprehensive and manageable, allowing you to prioritize resources effectively.

Step 2: Gather Data

Website Analysis: Your website is often the first point of contact between your brand and potential customers, making its performance critical. Utilize tools like Google Analytics, SEMrush, or Ahrefs to gather quantitative data on your website's performance. Focus on key metrics such as:

- **Traffic:** Assess overall traffic and segment by source (organic, direct, referral, etc.).
- **Bounce Rate:** Identify pages with high bounce rates to understand where users are disengaging.
- **Time on Site:** Evaluate how long visitors stay on your site, indicating engagement levels.
- **Conversion Rates:** Track how effectively your site is turning visitors into leads or customers.
- **Technical Performance:** Assess page load times, mobile responsiveness, and site architecture to ensure a smooth user experience.

Qualitatively, review your site's design, navigation, and content. Is the design aligned with your brand identity? Is the content explicit, engaging, and informative? Is the site easy to navigate? These elements play a crucial role in user experience and overall effectiveness.

Social Media Audit: Social media is a powerful tool for brand visibility and customer engagement. Conduct a thorough review of your social media profiles across platforms such as LinkedIn, Instagram, Twitter, and Facebook. Key metrics to analyze include:

- **Engagement:** Measure likes, shares, comments, and overall interaction with your posts.
- **Follower Growth:** Track the growth rate of your followers and analyze patterns.
- **Content Reach:** Evaluate the visibility of your content and its effectiveness in reaching your target audience.
- **Brand Mentions:** Monitor brand mentions and sentiment to gauge public perception.

Additionally, assess the consistency of your messaging, visual identity, and tone across platforms. Ensure that your social media presence aligns with your overall brand strategy and resonates with your audience.

Content Evaluation: Content is at the heart of digital engagement, serving as a vehicle for both information and conversion. Review the quality, relevance, and effectiveness of your content across all digital channels. Consider the following:

- **Relevance:** Is your content addressing the needs and interests of your target audience?
- **SEO Effectiveness:** How well does your content rank for relevant keywords? Ensure that your content is optimized for search engines.
- **Engagement:** Analyze how your audience interacts with your content—are they sharing it, commenting on it, or simply bouncing away?
- **Frequency and Freshness:** Regularly updated content keeps your audience engaged and signals to search engines that your site is active and relevant.

A comprehensive content audit should also include an assessment of your content's diversity (blogs, videos, infographics, etc.), its alignment with your marketing goals, and its performance in driving traffic and conversions.

Online Advertising Review: Digital advertising can be a significant driver of traffic and conversions, but only if it's effectively managed. Review the performance of your online ad campaigns using metrics such as:

- **Reach and Impressions:** Assess how many people are seeing your ads.
- **Click-Through Rate (CTR):** Evaluate the percentage of viewers who click on your ads.

- **Cost-Per-Click (CPC):** Determine the cost-effectiveness of your ad spend.
- **Conversion Rate:** Measure how many clicks are resulting in desired actions (e.g., purchases, sign-ups).
- **Return on Investment (ROI):** Calculate the overall profitability of your ad campaigns.

Examine whether your ad targeting is accurate and whether your creative assets (visuals, copy) are compelling enough to drive engagement. Additionally, consider whether your ads are aligned with your overall brand message and audience expectations.

Competitor Benchmarking: To gain a competitive edge, it's essential to understand how your digital presence compares to that of your key competitors. Perform a competitive analysis focusing on the following:

- **Market Positioning:** How does your brand's digital presence stack up against competitors?
- **Content Strategy:** What type of content are your competitors producing, and how is it performing?
- **Social Media Engagement:** Compare social media metrics to see where you may be falling behind or excelling.
- **Website Performance:** Use tools like SimilarWeb or Ahrefs to compare website traffic, backlinks, and rankings.

Competitor benchmarking allows you to identify gaps in your strategy and discover opportunities to differentiate your brand.

Step 3: Analyze and Interpret Findings

Identify Strengths and Weaknesses: With data in hand, the next step is to analyze and interpret your findings. Begin by identifying areas where your brand is performing well—these are your strengths. Simultaneously, pinpoint weaknesses that may be hindering your digital presence. Look for patterns in user behavior, such as pages with high exit rates, social media posts with low engagement, or ad campaigns with poor conversion rates.

A detailed analysis might reveal that while your website attracts significant traffic, the bounce rate is high, indicating a potential issue with user experience or content relevance. Or, you might find that your social media engagement is robust in one platform but lacking in another, suggesting a need for platform-specific strategies.

Conduct a SWOT Analysis: A SWOT (Strengths, Weaknesses, Opportunities, Threats) analysis provides a structured approach to synthesizing your audit findings.

- **Strengths:** In what areas are you doing well? This could include high website traffic, strong social media engagement, or effective content strategies.
- **Weaknesses:** Where are the gaps in your digital presence? Identify areas that require improvement, such as low conversion rates, inconsistent branding, or poor ad performance.
- **Opportunities:** What external factors can you leverage to enhance your digital presence? Look for trends in consumer behavior, emerging platforms, or gaps in the market that your brand could fill.
- **Threats:** What external factors could negatively impact your digital presence? Consider competitive pressures, changes in technology, or shifts in consumer expectations.

This analysis will provide a comprehensive understanding of your digital presence in relation to your business goals and the competitive landscape.

Step 4: Develop Actionable Recommendations

Prioritize Issues Based on Impact: Not all issues identified during the audit will have the same level of impact on your business. It's crucial to prioritize these issues based on their potential effect on your brand's performance. Focus on high-priority areas that offer the most significant opportunity for improvement. For instance, if your website has a high bounce rate on crucial landing pages, addressing this issue should be a top priority.

Consider creating a matrix that ranks issues by their urgency and impact, helping you allocate resources efficiently. High-impact, low-effort tasks should be addressed immediately, while high-impact, high-effort tasks can be planned for in the medium to long term.

Strategic Planning: Once priorities are set, develop a detailed roadmap to address the weaknesses and capitalize on the strengths identified. Your strategic plan should include:

- **Specific Actions:** Define the steps needed to address each issue. For example, if social media engagement is low, particular actions might include refining your content strategy, increasing post frequency, or experimenting with new types of content.
- **Timelines:** Establish realistic timelines for implementing each action. Prioritize quick wins that can provide immediate results while planning for longer-term initiatives.
- **Metrics for Success:** Determine how you will measure the success of each action. For instance, if the goal is to improve website conversion rates, metrics might include increased form submissions, product purchases, or sign-ups.

The strategic plan should be detailed enough to guide implementation while remaining flexible to adapt to changing circumstances or new insights.

Step 5: Implement Changes and Monitor Progress

Execute the Plan: With a clear roadmap in place, it's time to put your plan into action. Begin implementing the changes as outlined, focusing on the areas with the highest priority. This may involve:

- **Website Optimization:** Improving site speed, enhancing mobile responsiveness, updating content, and refining user navigation.
- **Social Media Strategy:** Adjusting content, frequency, and engagement tactics to better connect with your audience.
- **Advertising Adjustments:** Refining targeting, creative assets, and budget allocation to maximize ROI.

Ensure that all teams involved in the implementation are aligned with the plan and understand their roles in executing it.

Monitor and Adjust: Implementation is not the end of the process—it's an ongoing cycle of monitoring, learning, and adjusting. Continuously track the performance of your digital presence using the metrics defined in your strategic plan. Use analytics tools to measure the impact of your changes and make data-driven adjustments as needed.

Regularly review progress against your goals. If specific strategies are not delivering the expected results, be prepared to pivot and experiment with alternative approaches. The key is to remain agile and responsive to what the data are telling you.

Step 6: Regularly Review and Update

Make It an Ongoing Process: A digital presence audit is not a one-time task. The digital landscape is constantly evolving, with new platforms emerging, algorithms changing, and consumer behaviors shifting. To stay competitive, your brand must regularly review and update its digital assets.

Establish a routine for conducting mini-audits, quarterly or biannually, to ensure that your digital presence remains aligned with your business objectives. These periodic reviews will help you stay ahead of trends, address issues before they become significant problems, and continuously optimize your digital strategy.

Stay Ahead of the Curve: Regular audits will not only help you maintain a solid digital presence but also position your brand to capitalize on new opportunities as they arise. By staying ahead of the curve, you can ensure that your brand remains relevant, engaging, and competitive in an ever-changing marketplace.

Conducting a comprehensive digital presence audit is essential for business executives looking to optimize their brand's online performance. By following this expert-led framework, you can gain a deep understanding of your current digital footprint, identify areas for improvement, and develop a strategic plan that drives growth and enhances customer engagement. Remember, understanding where you stand today is the first step to building an impactful awareness strategy at the top of your digital consumer funnel.

Know the Customer Flow

Identifying a Problem

The first step in the consumer decision-making process is when your potential customers recognize a need—whether it's for a product or service. This need could be triggered internally, like hunger or a change in lifestyle, or externally by marketing and advertising efforts. As a business executive, it's crucial to understand that once this need is identified, consumers will begin searching for ways to fulfill it. Your role is to strategically influence this initial stage by creating marketing campaigns that highlight potential problems or opportunities that your product or service can address. In today's digital landscape, your marketing efforts should focus on engaging consumers with content that educates them, helping them recognize a need they might not have been aware of before. By doing so, you can effectively guide them to start their journey in the purchase decision process with your brand in mind.

Information Search

Once a consumer recognizes a need, their next step is to gather information about how to satisfy it. This is where they'll begin exploring their options, relying on both their own experiences and external sources like search engines, customer reviews, and social media. As a digital marketer, your job is to make sure your brand is visible and providing the information they're looking for during this critical stage. You need to strategically plan your content across various channels—blogs, webinars, videos, and social media posts—to position your brand as a trusted source. Additionally, incorporating consumer-generated content, such as customer reviews or testimonials, can be a powerful tool, as consumers tend to trust the experiences of others more than direct messaging from businesses.

Capitalizing on the Digital Search

In the digital age, search engines are often the first place consumers turn to when researching their options. Being present in these search results is vital. Your strategy should ensure that your brand is easily discoverable through SEO and paid search efforts. But it doesn't stop there—understanding which digital avenues your target audience uses is key. Whether it's YouTube videos, online reviews, or personal referrals, your content needs to be where your consumers are, ready to provide them with the information they need at the right time. By doing so, you're not only meeting them where they are in their decision-making process; you are also significantly increasing simultaneously the chances that they'll choose your brand when they're ready to make a purchase.

Optimizing Your Consumer's Discovery

By thoroughly evaluating and optimizing your online assets, you equip your brand with the insights needed to connect more effectively with digital consumers at every touchpoint. When your digital presence is aligned with consumer expectations, you are better positioned to capture attention, engage meaningfully, and leave a lasting impression. An audit helps you identify and correct weaknesses—whether it's a poorly optimized website, inconsistent social media messaging, or underperforming content—that might otherwise prevent your brand from reaching its full potential. By addressing these issues, you create a seamless and compelling brand experience that resonates with your target audience.

Moreover, a comprehensive audit enables you to discover new avenues for visibility. Whether through refined social media strategies, more targeted online advertising, or content that truly speaks to your audience's needs, the insights gained from a digital presence audit allow you to strategically position your brand where it matters most. This proactive approach ensures that your efforts to raise awareness are not just scattered attempts but are driven by data, targeted precision, and a deep understanding of your audience's digital behaviors.

Ultimately, by leveraging the findings from a successful audit, your brand can amplify its reach, engage with the right consumers, and build a robust online presence that not only attracts attention but also fosters loyalty. This sets the stage for sustained growth and positions your brand as a leader in the competitive digital marketplace.

Social Media

If you're not leveraging social media to its fullest potential, you're missing out on a massive opportunity to connect with consumers and drive brand awareness.

First off, consider this: Nearly **half** of consumers discover new brands through social media feeds. That's right—49 percent of global Internet users cite social media as a primary channel for finding new products and brands. This is a clear indicator of how pivotal social platforms have become in introducing consumers to brands they might not have encountered otherwise (Hootsuite 2023). For executives, this means your social media strategy isn't just about maintaining a presence—it's about being proactive in brand discovery.

But social media's influence doesn't stop there. It also plays a crucial role as a research tool. In fact, **54 percent** of social media users actively use these platforms to search for and research products. Consumers today are savvy; they're not just scrolling—they're investigating. This behavior positions social media as a vital element in the awareness stage of the consumer journey. If your brand isn't optimized for this type of interaction, you're potentially leaving a lot of value on the table.

And here's where it gets even more interesting—**71 percent** of consumers who have a positive experience with a brand on social media are likely to recommend it to others. This stat really drives home the power of social media in not just raising awareness but also fostering organic word-of-mouth promotion (Sprout Social 2023). Think of it as a modern-day referral network, where a single positive interaction can amplify your brand's visibility exponentially through peer-to-peer endorsements.

In summary, if you're aiming to drive brand awareness, social media isn't just an option—it's a necessity. The data back this up, showing how these platforms can introduce your brand to new audiences, serve as a key research tool, and even turn satisfied customers into brand advocates.

Influencers

No, you can't always hire a Mr. Beast or Kardashian. However, you can find authentic influencers, whether paid or unpaid, to help elevate the awareness of your brand. I have heard companies ask if it's really for them or not. It should be more about, should you versus could you. Any brand could, but *should* is the optimal word. Influencer marketing is not the saving grace for all brands.

By working with influencers who have loyal followers, you can introduce your brand to a broader audience in a way that feels genuine and relatable. People tend to trust recommendations from influencers they follow more than traditional ads, making it an excellent tool for reaching new customers and driving brand discovery.

However, it's vital for you to approach influencer marketing thoughtfully. You should choose influencers whose followers match your target market and whose style fits with your brand's message. Authenticity is critical; consumers can quickly tell if an endorsement doesn't feel genuine. Focus on building real, long-term partnerships with influencers who genuinely believe in your brand. This helps ensure that your message comes across in a way that feels trustworthy and effective.

Mobile Marketing

We all know how important mobile is, but what really matters is how you use it to connect with your audience. First impressions are everything, especially on mobile, where users decide in seconds whether to engage or move on. Over **57 percent of consumers** use mobile retail apps to find more information about a product or service, with many proceeding to make purchases directly through these apps (MoEngage 2023). Additionally, **70 percent of smartphone users** rely on their devices to gather information that influences their in-store purchases (Think with Google 2016). These statistics underscore the importance of having a well-optimized mobile presence—not just for initial brand discovery but also for impacting purchase decisions at critical moments.

If your mobile experience isn't fully optimized—whether through apps or mobile-friendly websites—you risk missing out on substantial opportunities to engage with potential customers when they are most primed to learn about and purchase your products. Ensuring that your mobile channels are accessible, seamless, and intuitive is critical to capturing and retaining consumer interest.

Know Your SEO

I cannot emphasize enough that while outbound marketing tactics such as mobile, influencer, and social media marketing may develop an excellent acquisition strategy for you, the foundational need to understand how you rank on Google Search outweighs anything you just read. By sheer need, not just desire, you need to rank as high on search engines as possible. I know it's challenging. Depending on your business, you could have dozens, hundreds to thousands of website competitors, all yearning for that top spot, yet alone, even on the first page of Google Results.

Let me start this by saying, though, that you will NEVER always be the top link. It's downright impossible to be in the top spot and hold it like a sealed brick to your home. However, you can continuously focus on being as high up as possible. This is where managing your **Search Engine Optimization (SEO)** really matters.

SEO is the practice of enhancing your website's visibility on search engines like Google. When done effectively, SEO helps your site rank higher in search results, making it easier for potential customers to find you. It involves optimizing your content and website structure and using relevant keywords that your target audience is searching for. The goal is to attract more organic (nonpaid) traffic to your site, which can lead to increased brand awareness, leads, and sales. In essence, SEO ensures that when people are looking for what you offer, they find you first.

Keyword Research and Analysis

Your goal should always be to rank high on a SERP or Search Engine Results Page. It all starts with effective management of knowing the keywords and phrases consumers and potential consumers use to find you online. It begins with Keyword Research and Analysis. It involves identifying and evaluating the specific words and phrases (keywords) that potential customers use when searching for products, services, or information related to your industry. This process helps you align your website content with what your target audience is searching for, thereby increasing your chances of appearing in search engine results and driving more organic traffic to your site (Figure 3.3).

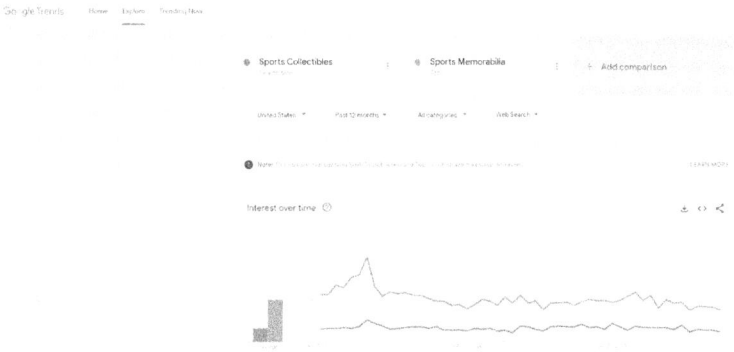

Figure 3.3 Google trends SEO analysis

For example, if you run an online sports collectibles store, you'd want to know what keywords collectors are using to find items like autographed baseballs or vintage trading cards. By targeting these keywords, you can ensure that your products are more easily found by those who are actively searching for them. Below is the ideal framework for conducting keyword research and analysis, keeping the sports collectible store theme for example sake.

- **Define Your Goals:**
  1. Start by determining what you want to achieve with your keyword research. Are you aiming to increase overall traffic, boost sales in specific categories, or attract a niche audience? Your goals will dictate the direction of your keyword strategy. For instance, an online sports memorabilia store might focus on keywords that target high-value collectors or fans of specific sports teams.
- **Identify Your Audience:**
  1. Understanding your target audience is essential. Consider who they are, what they're interested in, and how they search online. For a business, this might mean identifying whether your audience is looking for budget-friendly options or rare, high-end collectibles. Knowing your audience helps you select keywords that resonate with their search habits.

- **Brainstorm Seed Keywords:**
  1. Begin by listing broad terms related to your products or services. These "seed" keywords are the foundation of your research. For an online sports collectibles store, seed keywords might include "buy sports memorabilia," "autographed jerseys," or "vintage sports cards."
- **Use Keyword Research Tools:**
  1. Utilize tools like Google Keyword Planner, Ahrefs, SEMrush, or Moz Keyword Explorer to expand on your seed keywords. These tools will provide data on search volume and keyword difficulty and suggest related keywords. For instance, from the seed keyword "vintage sports cards," you might uncover associated terms like "rare baseball cards" or "1970s basketball cards."
- **Analyze Competitor Keywords:**
  1. Investigate the keywords that your competitors are ranking for. Tools like Ahrefs or SEMrush can help you identify these keywords. For example, a competitor in the sports memorabilia market might rank well for terms like "signed NFL helmets" or "Michael Jordan–autographed basketballs." Understanding this can help you identify opportunities or gaps in your own keyword strategy.
- **Evaluate Keyword Metrics:**
  1. Focus on three main metrics: search volume (how often a keyword is searched), keyword difficulty (how hard it is to rank for that keyword), and relevance (how closely the keyword aligns with your products or services). For a sports collectibles store, they might prioritize keywords like "buy autographed sports jerseys" if they have a good balance of search volume and competition.
- **Prioritize Keywords:**
  1. Based on your analysis, prioritize a mix of high-volume keywords for broader reach and long-tail keywords for more targeted, intent-driven traffic. For example, while "sports memorabilia" is a broad keyword, "Tom Brady–signed

football" could be a long-tail keyword that attracts highly motivated buyers.

- **Incorporate Keywords Strategically:**
  1. Use your chosen keywords naturally throughout your web-
     site, including in titles, meta-descriptions, headers, product
     descriptions, and blog posts. For example, a blog post on
     "Top 10 Most Valuable Signed Baseballs" can effectively target
     specific keywords while providing valuable content to your
     audience.

- **Monitor and Adjust:**
  2. SEO is an ongoing process. Regularly monitor your keyword
     performance using tools like Google Analytics and Search
     Console. Track changes in rankings, traffic, and conversions
     and be ready to adjust your strategy. For example, if a keyword
     like "vintage NFL helmets" is driving traffic but not convert-
     ing to sales, you may need to refine your content or focus on
     more specific terms like "Hall of Fame signed helmets."

By following this framework, businesses can conduct adequate keyword research and analysis that aligns with their goals, drives meaningful
traffic, and ultimately enhances sales.

Manage Your Google Quality Score

When meeting many digital executives, I find it fascinating that some of
them have never even heard of this. Or, maybe you yourself have heard
of it but don't really know how to manage it. Let's break it down in either
case (Figure 3.4).

Google's Quality Score is a critical metric that influences the performance and cost-effectiveness of your paid search campaigns. Quality
Score is Google's rating of the relevance and quality of your keywords,
ads, and landing pages. It's measured on a scale from 1 to 10, with 10
being the highest. A higher Quality Score can lead to lower costs per click
(CPC) and better ad positions, making it an essential factor for optimizing your search campaigns.

Quality Score

Figure 3.4 Quality score

Critical Factors Affecting Quality Score

- **Click-Through Rate (CTR):**
  - ○ **Importance:** CTR is the most significant component of the Quality Score. It measures how often people click on your ad after seeing it. A high CTR indicates that your ad is relevant to the searchers, leading Google to view it favorably.
  - ○ **Improvement Tips:** Write compelling ad copy that aligns with the user's search intent, use targeted keywords, and include strong calls to action (CTAs).
- **Ad Relevance:**
  - ○ **Importance:** Google assesses how closely your ad matches the intent behind a user's search query. Ads that are more relevant to the keywords will receive a higher score.
  - ○ **Improvement Tips:** Ensure your ads are tightly aligned with the keywords in your ad groups. Avoid generic ads that don't specifically address the searcher's query.
- **Landing Page Experience:**
  - ○ **Importance:** Google evaluates the quality and relevance of the landing page that users are directed to after clicking on your ad. A better landing page experience can significantly boost your Quality Score.
  - ○ **Improvement Tips:** Optimize your landing pages by ensuring they load quickly, are mobile-friendly, and offer valuable,

relevant content that matches the user's intent. The page should also be easy to navigate and include clear CTAs.

- **Keyword Relevance:**
  - ○ **Importance:** Your keywords should closely match the terms users are searching for—the more relevant your keywords, the higher your Quality Score.
  - ○ **Improvement Tips:** Conduct thorough keyword research and group similar keywords together in ad groups. Use negative keywords to filter out irrelevant traffic.

Strategies to Manage and Improve Quality Score

- **Continuous Optimization:**
  - ○ Regularly review and optimize your ads, keywords, and landing pages. Use A/B testing to refine your ad copy and landing pages to see what resonates best with your audience.
- **Refine Ad Copy:**
  - ○ Make sure your ad copy is relevant to the keywords in the ad group and provides a clear value proposition. Include the keyword in the ad text to increase relevance.
- **Enhance Landing Pages:**
  - ○ Ensure your landing pages provide a seamless experience that matches the ad's promise. This includes fast load times, mobile optimization, and content that fulfills the user's needs.
- **Monitor Keyword Performance:**
  - ○ Regularly check the performance of your keywords. Pause or adjust bids on low-performing keywords that are dragging down your Quality Score.
- **Use Google's Tools:**
  - ○ Utilize tools like Google Analytics and Google Ads' built-in diagnostics to gain insights into your Quality Score and identify areas for improvement.

By focusing on these critical factors and continuously optimizing your campaigns, you can improve your Quality Score, leading to more effective and efficient search advertising efforts.

The AI in All This

Artificial Intelligence (AI) is becoming a game-changer in how businesses connect with consumers, especially at the awareness stage of the digital marketing funnel. This is the phase where consumers first come across your brand, and AI plays a crucial role in making that first impression count. Think of AI as the engine that drives personalized, timely, and relevant interactions with potential customers, helping to ensure that your brand is noticed by the right people at the right time.

One of the most potent ways AI contributes to awareness is through personalized content delivery. AI analyzes vast amounts of data about user behavior and preferences, allowing businesses to create targeted ads and recommendations that resonate with specific audiences. For example, if someone has been browsing for vintage sports memorabilia, AI can ensure that they see ads for your store's latest autographed baseballs or rare trading cards, making your brand more relevant and attractive to them.

But it's not just about ads. AI also enhances how you target your audience in the first place. By processing demographic, behavioral, and contextual data, AI helps you segment your audience more precisely. This means you're not just throwing your marketing efforts out into the void; you're focusing on those who are most likely to be interested in your products. It's like having a digital concierge who knows precisely what your customers want before they even start looking.

AI also shines in content creation and optimization. Tools powered by AI can generate engaging content—like blog posts or social media updates—tailored to what your audience is searching for. Plus, AI can help you identify the best keywords for SEO, ensuring your content gets noticed in search engine results. This is especially important as more consumers use voice search, where AI can optimize content to match the natural language people use when speaking their queries.

Key Points

- Having great products and prices isn't enough; ensuring your brand is relevant and easily discoverable is crucial for success.

- Successfully balancing efforts between acquiring new customers and retaining existing ones is essential for sustainable business growth.
- Making a strong and immediate first impression in digital interactions is vital due to consumers' limited attention spans.
- Continuous adaptation and innovation are necessary for brands to be discovered.

As We Move Ahead

The top of the funnel is just the tip of the iceberg, as they say. Mastering awareness is essential to even get the consumers' foot into your digital door. As expressed, it is a lot of hard work, diligence, and decision-making. However, the challenge is now even greater. How do we create interest once we have them inside the door? That's what the next chapter is all about.

CHAPTER 4

Piquing the Interest, Nurturing Engagement

Your most unhappy customers are your greatest source of learning.

—Bill Gates

Chapter Overview

We are in a world of options. Your consumers have you, your competitors, and even non-competitors to choose from. Taking the next step of the digital funnel is ensuring that you have a message, incentive, and, ultimately, a value you can demonstrate to engage your digital consumer to move further with you. You got them in your digital door—and now it is time to get them to think. We are now in the consideration psychological state of the consumer, to really understand their learning styles, attitudes, and values. This chapter will orient these factors with a connection to digital strategies.

Consideration Phase

Kotler (2016) stated "Marketing is not the art of finding clever ways to dispose of what you make. It is the art of creating genuine customer value." This is core to the consideration phase of the funnel. Keyword, value. The consideration phase is a pivotal stage in the consumer journey where potential customers move beyond mere awareness and start actively evaluating their options. At this point, they are doing more than just glancing at products—they are diving into comparisons, scrutinizing features, benefits, pricing, and even the reputation of different brands. Consumers are assessing which product or service aligns most closely with their unique needs and preferences. This stage is where they decide whether what you offer truly meets their expectations, making it crucial for marketers to understand the importance of standing out. If your brand does not clearly communicate why it is the best choice, you risk losing the consumer to a competitor who does.

To succeed in this phase, it is not enough to simply have a great product or competitive pricing; you need to articulate your value proposition in a way that resonates with your target audience. This means going beyond the basics and offering rich, informative content that not only highlights the strengths of your product but also addresses any potential questions or concerns the consumer might have. With so many alternatives available, your goal is to differentiate yourself by demonstrating why your product or service is the best option. By effectively communicating your value, you not only attract consumers but also build the trust and confidence needed to convert them into loyal customers.

Piquing the Interest

Defining your value proposition is the moment of piquing consumer interest. Not the other way around. I have seen the faults of some digital marketers' thinking that we know our value and, therefore, only those quality consumers will truly understand it. No, you are proposing with each digital interaction what you perceive your value proposition to be. The consumer has the power to dictate whether they have interest in your value and will define it for you. It is through this mindset that the best digital strategies can flourish. You must first educate yourself and truly learn various factors about your consumers. This includes learning styles, attitudes, and value systems of your consumers.

Learning Styles

For a digital marketer, knowing the basics of consumer behavior and learning styles is key to creating strategies that really connect with your audience. When you understand how people learn and make decisions, you can craft content and campaigns that resonate more deeply, whether it is using social proof to build trust or consistently reinforcing your brand's value. It is about meeting your customers where they are and guiding them through their buying journey in a way that feels natural and compelling. This knowledge can be a game-changer in turning potential customers into loyal ones. Focusing on a couple of key theories helps in this practice.

Social Learning Theory (Observational Learning Theory):
According to Bandura (1971), this theory posits that individuals learn new behaviors, attitudes, and emotional reactions primarily by observing, imitating, and modeling the actions of others within a social context. In the consideration phase of the digital consumer funnel, consumers are actively gathering information and evaluating their options. They are not just looking at your product; they are also paying attention to what others are saying about it. When consumers see influencers, peers, or trusted sources endorsing your product online, it plays a significant role in their decision-making process. This is why leveraging social proof—like reviews, testimonials, and influencer partnerships—is so important during this phase. By highlighting positive examples of others using your product and benefiting from it, you can sway potential customers in your favor as they weigh their options.

Classical Conditioning Theory: This theory, also known as Pavlovian conditioning, is a learning process in which a neutral stimulus becomes associated with a stimulus that naturally produces a reflexive response (Pavlov, 1927). During the consideration phase, consumers are forming associations between your brand and the experiences they have with it online. If every time they encounter your brand they are met with appealing visuals, compelling content, or a memorable brand experience, these positive associations will stick with them. In the digital context, this could be through consistently engaging social media posts, well-crafted e-mails, or an aesthetically pleasing website. These repeated positive interactions help position your brand more favorably in the consumer's mind, making them more likely to choose you over competitors as they move through the decision-making process.

Example: Online Consumer Booking Travel: Imagine a customer planning a trip to a new destination and comparing different travel brands online during the consideration phase. To leverage learning styles effectively, you could use **Social Learning Theory**

by featuring influencer reviews or user-generated content, such as videos or blog posts, where real travelers share their positive experiences with your brand. Seeing others enjoy their trips booked through your service can sway the customer's decision.

At the same time, you could apply **Classical Conditioning** by consistently presenting your brand alongside positive stimuli. For example, your website and ads could feature stunning visuals of the destination, calming music, and testimonials that emphasize seamless booking and exceptional customer service. Over time, the customer begins to associate these positive feelings with your brand, making them more likely to choose you over competitors. These strategies help build trust and create a strong, favorable impression, guiding the customer toward booking with your brand.

Addressing Needs

Now that you can identify the type of learner your consumer is, it is now time to generate the influence needed to enhance that interest. If you successfully find that connection point where the interest is hooked in, then it is time to build other influential feelings and cognitive factors with your consumer. These are the aspects of consumer behavior that are critical, such as building trust, security, and meeting needs or wants.

Abraham Maslow, an American psychologist, developed the Hierarchy of Needs, which is based on human psychological factors and helps us understand different levels of motivation, from necessities to more complex desires (King-Hill 2015). This framework is incredibly useful for you as a business executive, especially when it comes to building influence during the consideration phase of the digital funnel. Understanding Maslow's hierarchy allows you to address the diverse needs of your customers—whether they are looking for basic security or seeking a sense of belonging and self-esteem—making your brand more relevant and persuasive (Figure 4.1).

Procter & Gamble (P&G) effectively applied Maslow's hierarchy of needs by focusing on essential products that addressed consumers' heightened need for safety and security. They ramped up production and promotion of hygiene and cleaning products, ensuring that consumers felt confident in their choices during a time of uncertainty. P&G also

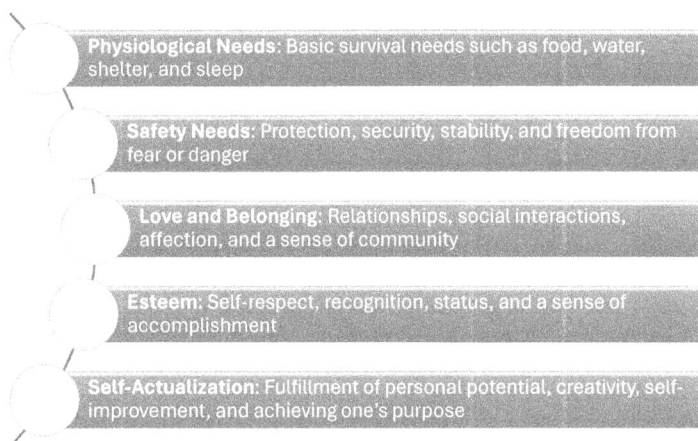

Figure 4.1 Maslow's hierarchy of needs

reinforced their brand's trustworthiness by launching campaigns that highlighted their support for healthcare workers and communities, tapping into higher-level needs like social belonging and self-esteem. This strategic approach helped P&G build significant influence during the consideration phase of the digital funnel, guiding consumers to choose their products and fostering deeper brand loyalty during the crisis.

By aligning your marketing strategies with where your customers are within this hierarchy, you can more effectively influence their decisions during the consideration phase. Whether it is by offering products that ensure their safety or services that enhance their self-esteem, you are building trust and authority in your brand. This not only helps in guiding customers through the funnel but also creates a deeper connection with them, as they see your brand as fulfilling their essential needs.

Adapting to Attitudes

Fishbein and Ajzen introduced the Theory of Planned Behavior in 1975, with Ajzen refining it further in 1991. This theory suggests that people's social behavior is influenced by specific circumstances, driven by intentions, and is often planned. For any behavior to manifest, there must be a clear intent behind it. As a digital marketing executive, this theory is highly relevant because it helps you understand the proactive traits of consumer behavior. The key components—attitude toward behavior,

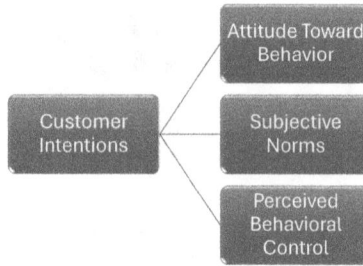

Figure 4.2 Theory of planned behavior

subjective norms, and perceived behavioral control—are crucial in shaping consumer intentions.(Figure 4.2).

What does this mean for you? It means you need to focus on consumer attitudes—how favorable or unfavorable they feel toward your brand. Some consumers come with preconceived notions, while others are open but need information and influence to build trust. To leverage this, ask yourself: What is the current perception of our brand? What online channels are consumers using to learn about us? And how can we use digital communication to positively influence their attitudes over time? By framing your digital strategy through the lens of consumer attitudes and subjective norms, you can better assess their intentions and guide their behavior toward making a purchase.

Here are three digital strategies that align with the Theory of Planned Behavior to help you understand and influence consumer attitudes during the consideration phase of the digital funnel:

1. **Leverage Targeted Content Marketing**
   Create and distribute content that speaks directly to the specific attitudes and concerns of your target audience. Use blogs, videos, and social media posts that address common questions or misconceptions about your brand or industry. By providing valuable, tailored content, you can positively influence consumer attitudes by positioning your brand as a trusted source of information. This helps build favorability and trust, crucial for guiding consumers through the consideration phase.

2. **Utilize Social Proof and Testimonials**

Incorporate social proof, such as customer reviews, testimonials, and case studies, into your digital channels. Display these prominently on your website, landing pages, and social media profiles. By displaying the positive experiences of others, you can influence the subjective norms around your brand, encouraging potential customers to view your offerings more favorably. This strategy leverages the concept that consumers are more likely to develop a positive attitude toward your brand when they see that others have had good experiences.

3. **Implement Retargeting Campaigns with Personalized Messaging**

   Use retargeting ads to reach consumers who have previously engaged with your brand but have not yet made a purchase. Tailor these ads to address specific attitudes or concerns they might have, based on their previous interactions. For example, if a consumer visited a product page but did not complete a purchase, your retargeting ad could highlight customer satisfaction or offer additional information that addresses common hesitations. By personalizing these messages, you can influence the perceived behavioral control, making it easier for consumers to feel confident in their decision to choose your brand.

   These strategies help you effectively shape consumer attitudes, making your brand more appealing during the crucial consideration phase of the digital funnel. Your goal as a digital marketer is to influence the intention that leads to a purchase decision. The Theory of Planned Behavior gives you a foundation to understand how digital consumers think, allowing you to craft digital experiences—through touchpoints, advertising, and service—that effectively influence intentions across different consumer segments. Embracing this theory will help you shape more effective strategies that align with the psychological processes driving consumer behavior.

Building Trust and Security

When it comes to building trust and security with your customers, understanding the **Trust Theory** is essential, especially in today's digital marketplace. This theory, which has been extensively studied in consumer behavior, highlights that trust is built on three core factors: competence, integrity, and benevolence (McKnight & Chervany 2001). As an executive, you need to ensure that your brand is seen as competent, meaning customers believe you can deliver on your promises. Integrity is just as critical; it is about being transparent, honest, and sticking to ethical practices. And then there's benevolence—showing your customers that you genuinely care about their well-being, not just your bottom line.

In the digital environment, you build this trust by focusing on secure website designs, clear privacy policies, and outstanding customer service. It is also reinforced by positive reviews and testimonials that signal to new customers that others have had safe and satisfying experiences with your brand. When you successfully cultivate trust, your customers feel secure in their transactions, which is crucial for encouraging repeat business and building long-term loyalty. Understanding and applying these elements of Trust Theory can give your brand a significant advantage in today's competitive digital landscape.

Example: Patagonia's Commitment to Transparency and Sustainability

Patagonia has established itself as a leader in building trust with its customers through its unwavering commitment to sustainability and transparency. In 2023, Patagonia launched an enhanced digital platform that allows customers to trace the environmental impact of their purchases. This "Footprint Chronicles" feature enables customers to see the environmental and social impact of each product, including information about where and how it was made, the materials used, and the working conditions of the people who produced it.

This initiative showcases Patagonia's integrity and benevolence, key components of Trust Theory. By being transparent about their supply chain and actively working to reduce their environmental impact, Patagonia not only builds trust but also aligns itself with the values of its customer base, who are increasingly concerned with sustainability.

Trust is also about authority in the offering. Trust is not just about being dependable; it is also about showing that you truly know your stuff and that your product genuinely meets the consumer's needs. You need to communicate this in a way that minimizes any doubts. But let us be real, consumers today are naturally skeptical. That is why it is crucial to provide both immediate, clear information and more detailed, secondary resources to back up your claims. This way, when consumers are evaluating your brand, you are not just meeting their expectations—you are building their confidence and sense of security in choosing you.

Three Key Digital Strategies

- **Detailed Product Pages with Educational Content:** Ensure your product pages are rich with detailed information. This includes not just the basic features but also educational content like how-to guides, explainer videos, and infographics. For example, if you are selling outdoor gear, include videos that demonstrate the product in action, showing its durability and effectiveness in real-world conditions. This not only conveys authority but also helps consumers feel confident that they are making an informed choice.
- **Leverage User-Generated Content and Reviews:** Integrate user-generated content, such as customer reviews, ratings, and testimonials, prominently on your site. Go a step further by encouraging customers to share photos or videos of themselves using the product. For instance, a clothing brand could feature customers showing off how they style their purchases. This peer validation helps reduce skepticism, as potential buyers see real people who have had positive experiences with your product.
- **Transparent and Accessible Customer Support:** Offer multiple channels for customer support that are easily accessible, like live chat, a detailed FAQ section, and responsive social media teams. Consider adding a chatbot that can answer common questions instantly or direct users to in-depth resources. For instance, if a customer is concerned about sizing, the chatbot could instantly link them to a detailed size guide or a video explaining how to measure properly. By being readily available to answer questions and resolve concerns, you further solidify the trust and authority of your brand.

These strategies are all about creating an environment where consumers feel informed and secure in their decision to choose your brand, which is key to building lasting trust and loyalty.

Holding Down the Engagement

Holding down engagement and nurturing it during the consideration phase of the digital funnel is all about staying connected with your potential customers as they weigh their options. This is the time when they are seriously thinking about making a purchase, but they need a little more information or assurance. Your goal is to keep them engaged by providing relevant, personalized content that helps them feel confident and valued.

Take **Sephora** as an example. When a customer browses makeup or skincare products, Sephora does not just hope they come back—they actively work to keep the interest alive. Sephora sends personalized recommendations through e-mails, offers virtual try-on tools, and even provides beauty tutorials that feature the products the customer has shown interest in. They might also offer exclusive discounts or free samples to sweeten the deal. By doing this, Sephora keeps the customer engaged, giving them valuable content that not only informs but also builds confidence in their potential purchase.

Another excellent example is **Kroger**. When a shopper shows interest in certain products, either online or through their loyalty program, Kroger keeps the engagement going by sending personalized offers and coupons based on their browsing or purchasing history. Kroger also uses its mobile app to suggest meal plans or recipes that include the items the customer has considered, tying the products into the shopper's daily life. This approach keeps customers engaged by showing how Kroger's products fit into their lifestyle, making it easier for them to choose Kroger when they are ready to make a purchase.

In both cases, Sephora and Kroger are doing more than just pushing for a sale—they are building a relationship by continually offering value and staying relevant during the customer's decision-making process. That is what it means to hold down engagement and nurture it—ensuring that as customers consider their options, your brand is the one they keep coming back to because you are meeting their needs in a thoughtful, personalized way.

Planning for Changes in Perception

Another factor in holding the engagement with consumers is the fact that their perception can change. Often, it is when we least expect it as well. Perception involves their viewpoint, opinion, and overall feeling when it comes to your offering, branding, or value proposition.

Framing Theory, developed by psychologists Amos Tversky and Daniel Kahneman (1981), is a powerful concept in both psychology and marketing that explains how the presentation of information—or the "frame"—can significantly influence consumers' perceptions and decisions. The core idea is that the same product or service can be perceived in entirely different ways depending on how it is framed. For instance, a discount can be presented as "20 percent off" or "Save $20," and although these two statements are mathematically equivalent, the framing might lead consumers to perceive one as more appealing than the other.

For you as a digital executive, understanding Framing Theory is crucial because it gives you the ability to strategically shape how consumers view your offerings during the consideration phase. This is the stage where potential customers are evaluating different options and deciding which brand to go with. By carefully choosing how to frame your product's benefits, pricing, or promotions, you can steer consumer perception in a way that makes your offering more attractive compared to the competition.

For example, if you are marketing a subscription service, framing a monthly fee as "less than the price of a coffee per day" might seem more affordable and relatable than just stating the total monthly cost. Similarly, highlighting "95 percent customer satisfaction" could be more persuasive than saying "5 percent dissatisfaction," even though both provide the same information. This strategic use of framing can make a significant difference in how consumers perceive the value and desirability of your product, influencing their purchase decision.

By leveraging Framing Theory, you can better align your messaging with how consumers naturally process information, helping you to guide them more effectively through the consideration phase and increase the likelihood of conversion.

Zorfas and Leemon's (2016) article from *Harvard Business Review* states:

> Shaping a customer experience by being precise about the emotional connections you're trying to build and investing in the touch points that drive these connections is a powerful way to increase customer value, and maximize the return on investment decisions and minimize the risk. Emotionally connected customers not only generate greater value, but in every interaction become more and more convinced that "this company gets me."

It emphasizes that businesses should clearly define the emotional responses they aim to evoke in customers and focus resources on the specific interactions or "touchpoints" that foster these connections. By doing so, companies can create deeper customer loyalty, which not only enhances customer lifetime value but also builds trust and alignment with the brand.

Emotionally connected customers tend to have a stronger bond with the company, leading to repeated purchases, positive word-of-mouth, and long-term engagement. Moreover, this approach helps businesses maximize their ROI by focusing on strategies that resonate deeply with their audience, minimizing the risk of ineffective or misaligned marketing efforts. Essentially, it's about creating a sense of understanding and relatability that makes customers feel that the company truly "gets" their needs and values.

Remember, you job is not to manipulate or shift perception based on smokes and mirrors. It is done with ethical intent, but with a strategic mind that you can *persuade perception.* Just as in-person selling, build the conversation through the offering, display the value, and close the deal. However, continuously planning for changing perception is the key.

AI in All This

As executives, you are always looking for ways to stay ahead of the curve, especially when it comes to understanding and leveraging the latest technology. One of the areas where AI is making significant strides is in the consideration phase of the digital consumer funnel. This is the stage where potential customers are evaluating their options—comparing products, reading reviews, and deciding if they should make a purchase. AI has the potential to transform how we engage with consumers during this critical phase, but it also comes with its own set of challenges that we need to navigate carefully.

Opportunities: Where AI Can Be Effective

- **Personalization at Scale**
  Imagine being able to deliver a unique, tailored experience to every potential customer who visits your website or interacts with your brand online. AI makes this possible by analyzing vast amounts of consumer data to provide personalized recommendations. This kind of personalization is not just a nice-to-have; it is becoming essential. Consumers now expect brands to understand their preferences and offer products that meet their specific needs. By leveraging AI, you can engage prospects more effectively, increasing the likelihood that they will choose your brand over the competition.
- **Enhancing the Customer Experience**
  Think about how many times you have wanted quick answers while considering a purchase. AI-powered chatbots and virtual assistants can provide immediate responses to consumer inquiries, making the consideration process smoother and faster. This does not just improve the customer experience—it can also accelerate their decision-making process, helping to close sales more efficiently.
- **Predictive Analytics**
  One of the most powerful aspects of AI is its ability to predict what a consumer might be interested based on past behaviors.

Imagine being able to anticipate a customer's needs before they even realize what they want. This is the kind of insight AI offers. By understanding and predicting consumer behavior, you can tailor your marketing efforts to be more relevant and timelier, driving higher conversion rates.

- **Optimizing Content Delivery**
AI can also help determine the best way to reach your audience during this consideration phase. Whether it is through personalized e-mail campaigns, targeted social media ads, or tailored website content, AI can identify the optimal channels and timing for your message. This ensures that your brand stays top of mind when consumers are making their purchasing decisions.

Challenges: What to Watch Out For

- **Data Privacy Concerns**
We cannot talk about AI without addressing data privacy. Consumers are increasingly concerned about how their data are being used, and with good reason. While AI relies on data to deliver personalized experiences, it is crucial to be transparent about how you are using this data and to ensure compliance with all relevant regulations. Building and maintaining consumer trust is key.

- **Algorithm Bias**
AI is only as good as the data it is trained on, and sometimes that data can introduce biases that affect the recommendations and decisions AI systems make. This can lead to negative consumer experiences or even damage your brand's reputation. It is important to regularly audit your AI systems to ensure they are fair, transparent, and free from bias.

- **Complexity of Integration**
Integrating AI into your existing marketing systems is not always straightforward. It requires investment in the right technology and talent. For some organizations, especially smaller ones, this can be a significant hurdle. It is important to weigh the benefits against the resources required and to approach integration in a phased, strategic manner.

- **Balancing Automation with Human Touch**
  While AI can automate many aspects of the consideration phase, it is crucial not to lose sight of the importance of human interaction. There is a fine line between leveraging AI to enhance the customer experience and relying too heavily on automation, which can lead to a lack of personal connection with your customers. The key is to use AI to *support*—and *not replace*—human engagement.

Conclusion: A Balanced Approach

AI offers incredible opportunities to enhance how we engage with consumers during the consideration phase of the digital funnel. However, it is not without its challenges. As executives, it is important to approach AI integration thoughtfully embracing its potential while being mindful of the pitfalls. By striking the right balance, you can use AI to improve customer engagement, build trust, and drive business growth.

Challenge of Consistency

As a digital executive, I understand the challenges of staying consistent in delivering the right content to consumers during the consideration phase. It is tough—managing multiple campaigns, juggling various channels, and ensuring that everything aligns with the customer's journey can feel overwhelming. I know the pressure to keep consumers engaged while also providing them with valuable and relevant information. There are times when it feels like I am constantly spinning plates, hoping none of them drop.

But I have learned that having a solid framework makes all the difference. For you, it starts with *effective planning*. You need to really understand where your customers are in their journey and map out what they need at each touchpoint. Set clear objectives for each phase, especially the consideration phase, where consumers are looking for that extra bit of information or reassurance. Ask yourself: What questions might they have? What concerns need addressing? Then, plan content that speaks directly to those needs—whether it is through personalized e-mails, targeted ads, or useful blog posts.

Next, you focus on *performance measurement*. It is not enough to just push content out; you need to know what is working and what is not. Set up key metrics to track—like engagement rates, click-through rates, and time spent on site—so you can see how well you are connecting with your audience. This helps you stay *agile*. If something is not resonating, you can pivot quickly and adjust your strategy to better meet your consumers' needs. Regularly reviewing these metrics ensures that you are not just consistent in your delivery but also effective.

By combining *thoughtful planning* with *ongoing measurement*, you can ensure that you are consistently delivering value to consumers during the consideration phase, keeping them engaged and moving closer to making a purchase.

Key Points

- The consideration phase is crucial because it is when consumers actively evaluate and compare products.
- Communicating a clear and compelling value proposition is essential to stand out during this phase.
- Understanding and leveraging consumer learning styles and behaviors can significantly enhance marketing effectiveness.
- AI can personalize and optimize consumer interactions, but it must be balanced with data privacy and human touch.

As We Move Ahead

This chapter looked at the consideration phase of the digital consumer funnel, where potential customers compared options to see if a product met their needs. It is paramount to communicate your values, understand consumer behaviors, and build trust through honesty and consistency. Next, we will focus on using data-driven insights to guide consumers through the funnel and turn information into actions that improve their journey.

CHAPTER 5

Data-Driven Insights: Turning Rocks into Gold

Without data, you're just another person with an opinion.
—W. Edwards Deming

Chapter Overview

The consumer journey is their digital footprint of information to our strategic success. The data, the gold mine of information we must understand the consumer, is at our helm to dig, investigate, and build upon. It is through the consideration phase that the gold mine is rich. Get your gloves and shovels because this chapter will get you in the mindset of data digging to decisions.

Data, Data, Data

In the consideration phase, where your digital consumer is browsing, clicking, viewing, sharing, and other actions, you gain some of the most essential information about them. The data are rich with added value for getting more familiar with their thoughts, feelings, attitudes, motivations, and triggers.

Data, as the building blocks of digital strategy, are more than just the ingredients to cook. You can build a subject-matter expertise and knowledge bank of information to leverage at your disposal. Especially during the consideration phase, the abundance of data is important for several reasons. According to a survey from McKinsey in 2023, companies that use customer behavioral data and insights outperform their competitors by 85 percent in sales growth. Now that's a positive statistic! Who doesn't want that kind of potential sales growth?

However the truth is, many digital marketers know that their company is not consistently data-driven. Keyword, consistent. You cannot just pick and choose digital strategies to be consumer-centric. It's got to be part of the organization DNA. As much as 87 percent of marketers say data are their company's most under-utilized asset (Invoca.com 2024). It's not even so much some companies don't know how to obtain data; it's about understanding how to use and/or leverage the data—specifically in the digital experience factor through web and mobile interactions and engagement with consumers.

Data-driven marketing transforms traditional approaches by customizing messages for each customer. By leveraging in-depth customer data, marketers can craft highly personalized experiences that connect more profoundly with consumers. This personalization not only strengthens customer relationships but also enhances our understanding of consumer behavior, leading to greater engagement and loyalty.

Every time a consumer clicks, views, or browses online, they provide real-time data incredibly valuable for your digital strategy. These actions are not just numbers—they are immediate insights into your customers' interests. By capturing this data as it happens, you can quickly adjust your marketing efforts, whether pushing a popular product, addressing a potential issue on your site, or tailoring offers to what the customer is actively looking for.

Real-time data also help you understand the consumer's journey more accurately. You can see which interactions lead to conversions and which might need improvement. This allows you to be more strategic in allocating resources, focusing on what is currently working. In today's fast-paced digital world, responding quickly and effectively is key to staying ahead of the competition and meeting your customers' needs.

Clicks, for instance, offer direct evidence of consumer interest and intent. When a consumer clicks on a particular link or advertisement, it signals their curiosity or need for more information, which can be tracked to understand which elements of your marketing efforts resonate. This action can be linked to subsequent behaviors, such as a purchase or sign-up, helping to attribute the effectiveness of specific marketing channels or messages in driving consumer decisions.

Views and browsing behavior, while more passive, are equally telling. The pages a consumer visits and the time spent on each page can reveal their level of engagement and areas of interest. For example, a consumer who spends considerable time on a product comparison page might be in the consideration phase, while one who repeatedly returns to a product page may be close to making a purchase decision. By analyzing these behaviors, companies can segment consumers more effectively and tailor their marketing strategies to match the consumer's position in the buying journey.

This holistic understanding of combining all these data points builds a strong **attribution** to our consumers. In digital consumer behavior, you need to understand how to connect attributes or characteristics to the consumers you serve. Building their profile is the foundation of where the input of these actionable data variables allows us to analyze behaviors to deliver optimized digital strategies.

Data Collection

Modern data collection processes in digital consumer behavior are all about capturing and analyzing every interaction a consumer has with your brand in real-time. This starts with tracking tools embedded in websites, apps, and social media platforms that automatically gather data whenever someone clicks on a link, views a product, or spends time on a particular page. These tools are sophisticated enough to not only log these actions but also provide context, like the time spent on a page, the path taken through your site, and even where the consumer came from, whether it is a search engine, an ad, or a social media post.

All of this data flow into centralized systems—often called Customer Data Platforms (CDPs)—which aggregate and organize it. These platforms allow you to see the full picture of a consumer's journey across different touchpoints. The real power comes from integrating these data with advanced analytics tools, which can segment consumers, predict behaviors, and even personalize experiences in real-time. More on this later.

Web Scraping Versus Web Crawling

Web data collection involves gathering information from websites to gain insights or drive business decisions. Two key methods in this process are web scraping and web crawling, which serve different purposes.

Web crawling is like sending a virtual robot to browse the Internet, automatically visiting websites to index content. Search engines, for instance, use web crawlers to scan the web, find new pages, and update their search results. This process is broad and systematic, covering substantial portions of the Internet.

Web scraping, on the other hand, is more targeted. It involves extracting specific data from a website, such as product prices, customer reviews, or inventory levels. Unlike crawling, which aims to collect general content, scraping is designed to pull out pieces of information from one or multiple websites, often to feed into databases or analytics tools.

For example, an e-commerce site might use web crawling to monitor competitors' sites for new product listings, ensuring their catalog stays competitive. Simultaneously, they could use web scraping to gather detailed pricing information and competitor customer reviews. This combined approach allows them to adjust their pricing strategies in real-time, keeping them ahead in a competitive market.

Behavioral Tracking

Behavioral tracking captures every user interaction on your digital platforms—a click, a scroll, or a purchase (Figure 5.1). These data are collected through tracking codes or cookies embedded in your website or app. Tools like Google Analytics then analyze this data, breaking it down to show patterns and trends. For example, you can see which pages users spend the most time on, where they abandon the site, and which paths lead to conversions.

Google Analytics 4 (GA4) provides detailed reports that help you dive deep into user behavior. It can show you the effectiveness of different marketing channels, the performance of specific content, and even user demographics. This insight allows you to make informed decisions on optimizing your site—improving the user journey, tweaking content to boost engagement, or refining your marketing efforts to target the right audience more effectively. By leveraging this data, you can continuously refine your digital strategy to meet customer needs better and drive business growth.

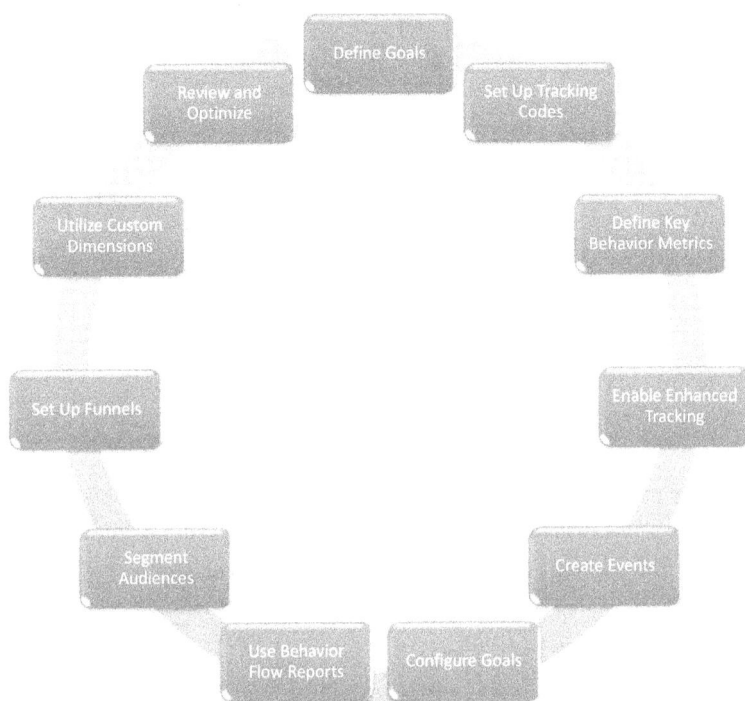

Figure 5.1 Behavioral tracking process

The Path and Patterns

Imagine you are observing how visitors move through your website—like tracking footprints in a digital store. This is what clickstream and pathing analysis are all about. **Clickstream** refers to a visitor's sequence of clicks as they navigate your site. **Pathing analysis** digs deeper into these click patterns to uncover the most common routes people take, where they might drop off, and which paths lead to conversions.

Analyzing these patterns lets you understand your digital consumer behavior more clearly. You will see what captures their attention, what frustrates them, and what leads them to act, like making a purchase or signing up for a service (Figure 5.2).

Clickstream and pathing analysis empower you to understand better and engage with your customers, driving business success.

Benefits	Challenges
Enhanced Customer Insights: You better understand what your customers want and how they behave, allowing you to tailor their experiences more effectively.	Data Overload: You might be overwhelmed with data, making it challenging to pinpoint the most critical insights without the right tools or expertise.
Improved Conversion Rates: By optimizing the paths that lead to successful actions, you can increase conversions and boost your bottom line.	Privacy Concerns: Handling consumer data responsibly is crucial. Any misstep could harm your brand's reputation.
Targeted Marketing: You can identify key touchpoints in the customer journey, enabling more personalized and effective marketing efforts.	Complexity in Interpretation: Understanding the nuances of consumer behavior can be tricky. Simplifying these insights for action requires experience and the right analytics support.

Figure 5.2 Benefits and challenges of pathing analysis

Digital Trends

A **digital trend** in consumer behavior refers to a noticeable pattern or shift in how consumers interact with digital platforms over time. These trends include increasing use of mobile devices for shopping, a preference for video content, or rising interest in personalized recommendations. Identifying and analyzing these trends is crucial because they reveal changes in consumer preferences, which you can leverage to stay ahead of your competitors. We often try to mirror the trends that are external to us.

You will see your competitor launch or implement a new digital experience, and we thrive in that need to be a part of it. This is the case. Being inspired by your competition is always valid. However, you cannot of course copy-cat. Remember, though, your digital consumer data are yours. Your inspirations from competition should be fueled by your desire to understand the digital trend and create your differentiators. Therefore, embrace the digital trend, and then learn your unique spin on how to optimize it.

Clickstream and pathing analysis are powerful tools to measure these trends. By tracking how visitors navigate your website, you can identify emerging patterns in their behavior. For instance, if you notice a growing number of users abandoning their carts on mobile devices, this could in-dicate a trend toward mobile shopping and highlight a potential friction point in your mobile experience.

Real-World Examples of Trend Analysis in Action

- **E-commerce Website Adjusting to Mobile Shopping Trend:** You run an online clothing store. Through clickstream analysis, you discover that an increasing number of users are browsing and shopping on mobile devices, but your conversion rates on mobile are lower than on desktop. Recognizing this trend, you optimize your mobile site—making it faster, easier to navigate, and more visually appealing. As a result, you might see a significant boost in mobile conversions, aligning your strategy with the ongoing trend of mobile-first shopping.
- **Streaming Service Responding to Content Consumption Patterns:** Imagine you operate a streaming service. Pathing analysis reveals that users who watch short video clips are more likely to subscribe to premium content after being recommended related videos. By identifying this trend, you can enhance your recommendation algorithm to prioritize short clips, leading to higher engagement and subscription rates. Additionally, adjust your marketing strategy to highlight the availability of short-form content to attract more users who prefer quick, digestible media.

You can continuously refine your digital marketing strategies by un-derstanding and responding to digital trends through clickstream and pathing analysis. Whether adapting to new consumer preferences, opti-mizing user experiences, or personalizing content delivery, these insights ensure your business remains relevant and competitive in the ever-evolving digital landscape.

Trends and Touchpoints to Retention

When moving digital consumers through the funnel, the real magic happens at the **touchpoints**—those crucial moments when a consumer interacts with your brand. By analyzing trends at these touchpoints, you can understand what drives consumers to advance to the next stage in their journey and optimize their experience to encourage that progression.

Touchpoints in the Funnel

1. **Establishing Touchpoints**

   First, it is important to map out the key touchpoints in your digital funnel. These include the initial landing page, product pages, the shopping cart, e-mail interactions, customer support chat, and post-purchase surveys. Each touchpoint represents an opportunity to move the consumer forward or lose them entirely.

2. **Analyzing Consumer Behavior at Each Touchpoint**

   Once you have identified these touchpoints, use trend analysis to dive into consumer behavior at each one. For instance, consumers who engage with a live-chat feature on the product page are more likely to proceed to purchase. Or you might notice that consumers who land on your site via a social media ad are dropping off quickly, indicating that the landing page must resonate with them.

   It would help if you thought more quantitatively here. The actual touchpoint data point is a record of a count. However, you need to connect the touchpoint to the content or intent you had initially. For example, if your banner was displayed to generate more content to educate your consumer, the click at that banner touchpoint showed further interest. The placement is also key. Focusing on the place of that touchpoint matters. Behaviorally, you can understand who is deeper engaged the more down the page they scroll or more time they spent on your website or digital campaign as an example.

   Gillian Moran, Laurent Muzellec, and Eoghan Nolan emphasize the strategic importance of "Moments of Truth" (MOTs) in the consumer journey, highlighting that these pivotal interactions between a customer and a brand can impact decision-making. In today's digital landscape, effectively managing these moments, particularly through integrating shared brand experiences and electronic word-of-mouth (e-WOM), is essential for influencing consumer behavior and maintaining competitive advantage (Moran et al. 2014). With that theoretical understanding, the need to evaluate touchpoints and moments as a source of directional truth is the key to success in this assessment.

3. **Optimizing Touchpoints Based on Insights**

   With these insights, the next step is optimizing each touchpoint to better guide consumers to the next stage.

   ○ **Landing Pages:** If trend analysis shows that your landing page has a high bounce rate, consider simplifying the design, clarifying the call to action (CTA), or ensuring the page content aligns better with the ads or search results that brought users there.

   ○ **Product Pages:** If consumers often spend time on product pages but do not add items to their cart, it might be worth enhancing these pages with more detailed product descriptions, user reviews, or comparison tools. This can help consumers make more informed decisions, increasing the likelihood of moving to the cart stage.

   ○ **Shopping Cart:** If cart abandonment is a trend, streamline the checkout process. Reduce the number of steps, offer guest checkout options, or communicate shipping costs early in the process. To encourage completion, you can also add urgency elements like low-stock alerts or time-limited discounts.

   ○ **E-mail and Retargeting:** Trend analysis can also inform how you interact with consumers post-touchpoint. For instance, if someone leaves items in their cart, a well-timed e-mail reminder or retargeting ad can bring them back to complete their purchase. Personalization plays a key role here, as customizing these messages based on the products they viewed or added to their cart makes the nudge more effective.

4. **Creating a Seamless Transition Between Touchpoints**

   Another critical aspect of optimizing touchpoints is ensuring a seamless transition from one to the next. For example, if a consumer reads a blog post on your site, the next logical step might be a CTA leading them to related products or services. If they engage with customer support, ensure that the interaction is smooth and that any issues they raise are quickly resolved, making them more likely to trust and purchase from you.

Seamlessness also means maintaining consistency in messaging and branding across all touchpoints. If a consumer experiences a disconnect between what they see in an ad and what they find on your landing page, they are likely to drop off. Aligning these touchpoints ensures a cohesive journey that builds trust and encourages progress through the funnel.

5. **Continuous Improvement and Adaptation**
Finally, trend analysis will be used for ongoing optimization. The digital landscape is constantly evolving, and so are consumer behaviors. Regularly monitor how consumers are interacting with your touchpoints and be ready to adjust. For instance, as mobile usage trends increase, you need to optimize touchpoints for mobile-first experiences. Integrating videos into key touchpoints could enhance engagement and conversion if video content becomes more popular.

By focusing on touchpoints and optimizing them based on trend analysis, you create a smoother, more intuitive journey for your consumers. This approach helps them move efficiently through the funnel and builds a more satisfying and engaging experience that encourages long-term loyalty.

Retention

Retention is about keeping your customers engaged and coming back for more; trend analysis is a key tool in achieving this. By identifying patterns in your customers' behavior, you can anticipate their needs, address potential issues before they escalate, and enhance their overall experience, improving retention rates.

Steps to Leverage Trend Analysis for Retention Optimization

- **Identify Key Behavioral Trends:** Use clickstream and pathing analysis to observe how customers interact with your site over time. For example, look for trends in how often they visit, what content or products they engage with, and where they drop off. Identifying these patterns allows you to understand what keeps them interested and what might cause them to leave (Figure 5.3).

Figure 5.3 Trend analysis for retention optimization

- **Pinpoint High-Retention Segments:** Analyze the behaviors of your most loyal customers to understand what keeps them coming back. Do they frequently use certain features, purchase specific products, or engage with types of content? You can focus on replicating these behaviors across your broader customer base by identifying these high-retention segments.

- **Address Common Drop-Off Points:** Pathing analysis can reveal where customers tend to drop off during their journey—whether it is a cumbersome checkout process, confusing navigation, or lack of relevant content. By recognizing these trends, you can make targeted improvements to remove these barriers, creating a smoother, more enjoyable experience that encourages customers to stay.

- **Personalize Engagement Strategies:** Use trend data to tailor your communication and engagement strategies. For instance, if a trend shows that customers are more likely to return when they receive personalized recommendations or offers, you can implement automated systems to deliver these at key moments. This personalized touch can significantly boost retention.

- **Monitor and Adjust in Real-Time:** Consumer behavior constantly evolves, so it is important to monitor trends continuously. Real-time analysis allows you to quickly identify shifts in behavior and adjust your retention strategies accordingly. For example, if a new trend shows a sudden interest in a specific product category, you can create targeted campaigns or special offers to capitalize on this interest.

Example: Subscription-Based Service

Consider a subscription-based service like a fitness app. Trend analysis reveals that users who engage with new workout content within the first week are significantly more likely to renew their subscriptions. To optimize retention, you could implement a strategy that pushes notifications or personalized e-mails highlighting new workouts to users during their first week. Additionally, you could offer incentives like a free personal coaching session for users who hit specific milestones early on, based on the trend data showing high retention rates among users who actively engage in their first month.

Example: E-commerce Business

For an e-commerce business, trend analysis might show that customers who participate in loyalty programs or leave reviews tend to make repeat purchases. To leverage this trend, you could enhance your loyalty program, offering more rewards or exclusive discounts and encourage review submissions with incentives. By aligning your retention efforts with these positive behavioral trends, you create a more compelling reason for customers to stay loyal to your brand.

Leveraging trend analysis to optimize retention is about proactively anticipating your customers' needs and addressing pain points before they become issues. By continuously monitoring trends, personalizing experiences, and removing barriers, you can create a customer journey that retains and delights, ensuring long-term loyalty and business growth.

AI in All This

Turning data into actionable insights is like turning raw ingredients into a delicious recipe—it takes the right process and tools. Through the data collection and capturing processes outlined in this chapter, you must understand how to optimize your strategic decision-making. Each of these interactions with your digital consumer leaves behind valuable data that tell you something about your customers' preferences, needs, and behaviors.

Once you have gathered all this data, the next step is to analyze it. This is where the right analysis tools and software come into play. These tools are designed to sift through the data and identify patterns—like noticing that customers who view a certain product are more likely to purchase if they also read reviews. These patterns are the "data-driven insights" that help you understand what works and what does not.

Because these insights are grounded in real customer behavior, they allow you to make smarter, more informed decisions. For instance, certain content, like how-to videos, is particularly effective at keeping customers engaged. Or you might learn that simplifying your checkout process can reduce cart abandonment. With these insights, you can tweak your strategies—which products to promote, how to design your website, or what kind of content to create—to better meet your customers' needs.

Training and Calibrating AI Models

Now, let us dive into how data play a crucial role in training and refining AI, or artificial intelligence. Think of AI as a super-smart assistant that can help you anticipate what your customers might want or automate repetitive tasks. But for AI to be effective, it needs a lot of data to learn from.

Imagine you are teaching someone to recognize different dog breeds. You would show them lots of pictures of dogs. The more they see, the better they get at telling one breed from another. AI works the same way. The more data you provide—like customer browsing habits, past purchases, and product preferences—the better the AI predicts what your customers might do next. It can even start suggesting personalized products or optimizing the timing of your marketing e-mails to boost engagement.

But it does not stop there. Just like someone might need to practice or get feedback to improve their skills, AI models must be calibrated or fine-tuned over time. This involves regularly checking how well the AI performs and adjusting based on new data. For example, if you notice more customers shopping on their phones, you will update the AI with this new data to continue making accurate predictions.

Why This Matters

Using data to generate insights and train AI is about more than just having fancy technology but understanding your customers. Instead of relying on guesses or assumptions, you use real, up-to-date information to see what your customers want and need. This leads to more personalized experiences, better marketing strategies, and stronger relationships with your customers.

Data are the fuel that powers your insights and AI tools. The more high-quality data you have, the better you can understand your customers and stay ahead in the digital world. By continuously refining your approach based on data, you ensure that your business remains responsive, relevant, and ready to meet the ever-changing needs of your customers.

Example: How Data-Driven Insights and AI Enhance Digital Consumer Behavior

Let us say you are an executive at an online fashion retailer. You have noticed that while you get a lot of website visitors, many of them need to make purchases. This is where data-driven insights and AI come into play to help you understand and improve digital consumer behavior.

Step 1: Collecting and Analyzing Data

First, you gather data from various touchpoints—website visits, product views, time spent on certain pages, items added to the cart, and checkout completions. You also track data from your e-mail campaigns, social media interactions, and customer service inquiries.

When you analyze this data, you notice a pattern: Customers who browse for more than 5 minutes and view multiple products often add items to their cart but leave without completing the purchase. This insight tells you interest, but something stops them from buying.

Step 2: Using AI to Personalize the Experience

With this insight, you use AI to personalize the shopping experience. You implement an AI-driven recommendation system that suggests similar or complementary products based on what each customer has viewed. For example, if a customer spends time looking at a particular dress, the AI might suggest matching shoes or accessories, which can entice them to make a purchase.

Moreover, you set up an AI-powered retargeting campaign. If a customer adds items to their cart but does not check out, the AI sends them a personalized e-mail a few hours later with a gentle reminder, including a limited-time discount to encourage them to complete the purchase.

Step 3: Calibrating AI Based on New Data

After implementing these changes, you keep monitoring the data. You notice that retargeting e-mails are particularly effective when sent within an hour of cart abandonment, rather than after a few hours. So, you fine-tune the AI to adjust the timing of these e-mails, increasing the chances of conversion.

Additionally, as mobile shopping grows, you update the AI models with new data to ensure the recommendations and retargeting work seamlessly on smartphones and tablets, making the experience as smooth for mobile users as it is on desktops.

The Result: Improved Consumer Engagement and Sales

You start seeing improvements by using data-driven insights to understand where your customers were getting stuck and leveraging AI to personalize and optimize their journey. Customers now find products they love more easily, receive timely reminders, and are more likely to complete their purchases. This not only boosts your sales but also enhances customer satisfaction and loyalty.

This example shows how data and AI work together to understand and influence digital consumer behavior. You create a more engaging and effective customer journey by analyzing data to spot patterns, using AI to personalize the shopping experience, and continuously fine-tuning your approach. This leads to better business outcomes—more sales, happier customers, and a stronger brand.

Key Points

- The consideration phase offers critical insights into consumer preferences through their browsing and clicking behaviors.
- Real-time data enable businesses to swiftly adapt their marketing strategies to match current consumer interests.
- Assessing touchpoints and moments provides clear visibility into the customer journey, highlighting conversion drivers and areas for improvement.
- Detailed consumer profiles built from data analysis empower more targeted and effective digital strategies.

As We Move Ahead

Focusing on the benefits of data during the consideration phase has been explained as being of upmost value to you. Through that process, there is another dynamic that must be considered. Trust. As you are collecting vast amounts of consumer data through all of their digital interactions, there is also your digital consumer desiring to feel secure and trustful in their interactions. This puts a spotlight that protecting their information and being ethical in its use is critical. The next chapter dives into these parameters in greater detail.

CHAPTER 6

Ethical Considerations: Safeguarding Consumer Trust

You've got to hold on to what we've got

—Bon Jovi

Chapter Overview

Bon Jovi's lyric captures the essence of this chapter, where we explore the critical importance of trust in the digital consumer world. In today's landscape, where personal data are shared constantly, safeguarding that information is a nonnegotiable for businesses. This chapter dives into the ethical responsibility that companies must protect consumer data, how to communicate transparently when things go wrong, and the role AI plays in preventing threats. We will break down how balancing legal compliance with a genuine commitment to privacy can build long-lasting consumer relationships. Trust is the foundation of it all, and, without it, everything falls apart.

Ethics in Digital Consumerism

When we talk about ethics in digital consumerism, we are discussing the moral principles that should guide your company's digital interactions with consumers. This goes beyond just avoiding deceptive practices—it is about building trust, protecting privacy, and ensuring fairness in a digital landscape where consumers are more aware and vigilant than ever before. The easiest consideration on why this matters is to just look at some examples where not upholding an ethical environment on data privacy can truly have a backlash to an organization.

Facebook and the Cambridge Analytica Scandal (2018)

One of the most prominent data privacy scandals was the Facebook–Cambridge Analytica situation. Back in 2018, it was revealed that Cambridge Analytica, a political consulting firm, had accessed data from over 87 million Facebook users without their permission. These weren't just any data—they used it to build detailed profiles on users to micro-target voters during political campaigns, including the 2016 U.S. Presidential election.

The story broke when a whistleblower came forward, and it caused massive outrage. Suddenly, people realized their personal information had been misused, and Facebook was caught in the middle. The financial hit was huge—Facebook's market value plummeted by over $100 billion in just a few days. More importantly, this scandal highlighted just how far behind Facebook was in protecting consumer data and being transparent. It served as a wake-up call for the tech industry on the importance of obtaining clear user consent before collecting or using personal data.

Equifax Data Breach (2017)

The Equifax data breach is another case where a major company mishandled consumer data, leading to massive fallout. In 2017, Equifax, one of the largest credit bureaus in the United States, suffered a breach that exposed the personal information of 147 million people. This included incredibly sensitive information like Social Security numbers, birthdates, and addresses. What made this breach even worse was how poorly Equifax managed it.

The breach happened months before it was made public, and their initial response was far from reassuring. The company's website for affected consumers was confusing and did not do much to calm the public. This was a prime example of how **not** to manage a data breach. Equifax ended up facing serious legal consequences, including a settlement of up to $700 million. The incident underlined how critical it is for companies to have strong data security measures in place and to be transparent with consumers when things go wrong.

These are just two prominent examples where ethics in digital consumer is not just protecting the data, but, more importantly, being transparent, communicative, and able to speak to the truth without sweeping it under the rug. That is the core of the ethical piece. Hacking, cyberattacks, and other unfortunate events occur. It is how we as digital marketers and business executives decide to communicate it during a time of PR crisis, which may matter more than the event itself.

Why Should You Care?

Understanding ethics in this context is crucial for several reasons. First, today's consumers are incredibly savvy. They can spot a dishonest practice from a mile away, and they are not afraid to call it out. Social media has given them a powerful voice, and one misstep can quickly snowball into a PR crisis. Second, regulations around digital consumer rights are tightening globally, and staying ahead of these changes can save your company from hefty fines and legal battles. But, more importantly, ethical practices build trust, and trust translates to brand loyalty—a currency far more valuable than any short-term gain.

Termly.IO (2024) stated that 94.1 percent of businesses believe you can achieve a balance between data collection for marketing and respecting customer privacy. This is a promising statistic with the emergence of this prioritization in your workplace. Keyword though is *believed*. That is the crux in some organizations. The concept of keeping consumer data private is an ethical and respectable notion. However, are you doing it correctly? That is the real question. Let us err on the side that the belief is true based on that statistic; if that is the case, then why all the fuss? Well, it comes down to a few key principles for you as a digital marketer.

Regulation

First, are you conducting these data privacy tactics because you fully believe in the privacy of your consumers or are you just trying to comply with data privacy regulations? Well, it should be a mix of both. We should *want* to protect our consumer data, while *needing* to comply with law and regulation. Let us talk about regulation for a moment.

Navigating data privacy laws is more crucial than ever. With consumers increasingly aware of their rights and governments tightening regulations, businesses must balance data-driven strategies with compliance. Three of the most impactful data privacy laws are the **General Data Protection Regulation (GDPR)**, **California Consumer Privacy Act (CCPA)**, and **Virginia Consumer Data Protection Act (VCDPA)**. Let us explore these laws and how your business can develop robust data privacy practices to comply.

1. **GDPR: Setting the Global Standard**
   The **General Data Protection Regulation (GDPR)**, enacted by the European Union in 2018, remains the benchmark for data privacy laws globally. It governs any company that processes the personal data of EU residents, regardless of where the company is based. Some key GDPR provisions include:
   - **Consent**: Businesses must obtain clear, affirmative consent from consumers before collecting personal data.
   - **Data Subject Rights**: Individuals have the right to access, correct, or erase their data and can request the transfer of their data to other service providers.
   - **Breach Notification**: Companies must notify authorities within 72 hours of becoming aware of a data breach.

   Managing GDPR Compliance: Businesses must prioritize **privacy by design**, ensuring that data protection is integrated in every step of operations. Implementing consent management tools and conducting regular data audits are essential to demonstrating compliance. Additionally, appointing a **Data Protection Officer (DPO)** may be required, depending on your company's data processing activities.

2. **CCPA: California Leads U.S. Privacy Initiatives**
   The **California Consumer Privacy Act (CCPA)**, which came into effect in 2020, was a landmark moment in U.S. data privacy law. Designed to give California residents more control over their

personal data, it applies to businesses operating in California or dealing with its residents. Key elements of the CCPA include:

- **Right to Opt-Out**: Consumers can request that businesses stop selling their personal data.
- **Right to Know**: Consumers can request information on the categories of data collected, the purpose for its collection, and third parties with whom the data are shared.
- **Right to Delete**: Consumers can ask for their data to be deleted, with some exceptions.

Managing CCPA Compliance: Transparency is key to CCPA compliance. Your business must provide clear and accessible methods for consumers to opt out of data sales and request information about their data. Regularly updating your privacy policies and ensuring that they clearly explain how data are used will build trust and protect your business from potential litigation.

3. **VCDPA: Virginia's Expanding Influence**

Virginia's **Consumer Data Protection Act (VCDPA)**, which went into effect in 2023, is another major American privacy law following in the footsteps of the CCPA. The VCDPA applies to businesses that control or process data of at least 100,000 consumers or derive more than 50 percent of their revenue from selling personal data. Like GDPR, VCDPA focuses on consumer rights and transparent data practices. Its key provisions include:

- **Consumer Rights**: Like GDPR, VCDPA gives consumers the right to access, correct, and delete their personal data, as well as the right to opt out of targeted advertising and the sale of their data.
- **Sensitive Data Protection**: Businesses must obtain consent before collecting or processing sensitive personal data, including data related to race, religion, health, and precise geolocation.
- **Data Protection Assessments**: Businesses are required to conduct regular assessments to ensure they are handling consumer data in a secure and compliant manner.

Managing VCDPA Compliance: The VCDPA emphasizes **consumer empowerment**, and businesses should ensure they have the infrastructure in place to handle consumer data requests. In addition, adopting **data minimization** practices—where businesses only collect data that are necessary for their operations—can help streamline compliance efforts. Conducting regular assessments of your data protection practices and implementing opt-out mechanisms for targeted advertising will also be critical.

Best Practices for Managing Data Privacy Across Laws

While each of these laws has unique requirements, there are overarching best practices your business can implement to manage compliance across different regulatory frameworks:

4. **Implement Data Governance**: Establish strong data governance frameworks that include internal policies on how data are collected, stored, and shared. Regular audits and risk assessments can help you identify areas for improvement.

5. **Prioritize Transparency**: Ensure that your privacy policies are clear and accessible to consumers. Avoid legal jargon and focus on making your data practices easy to understand.

6. **Use Data Minimization Techniques**: Only collect the data you need and ensure you have a clear business purpose for each data collection point.

7. **Stay Proactive**: As data privacy laws evolve, staying informed about upcoming changes will ensure your business remains compliant. For example, new regulations, such as the **Colorado Privacy Act (CPA)**, are coming into force, expanding data protection frameworks across the United States.

Managing data privacy in today's business environment requires more than just ticking off compliance boxes. It requires building a **privacy-first culture**, where protecting consumer data is integral to your operations. By following the principles of GDPR, CCPA, and VCDPA, your business can not only avoid legal pitfalls but also foster consumer trust—a crucial element for long-term success. Also, the global attention to the need for more data privacy regulation is not slowing down. According to Thales Group (2024), more than 120 countries have already addressed international data protection laws in some form to provide better protection for their citizens and their data. So, depending on where you are located and operating as you read this, what does your local legislation on this look like? I suggest reading up on it and having proper counsel to help comply.

Why Do Your Consumers Care?

As mentioned, your digital consumers are very savvy. We need to give them more credit about their acknowledgment on how and when their data are used than maybe we give them credit for. A Pew Research Center survey in 2019 highlighted that 62 percent Americans did believe they cannot go through their daily life without some form of their data being collected. The awareness is there. This statistic is even pre-pandemic, before the surge of digital interactions and business exponentially increased.

Consumers know their information is being collected. To consumers, it is just the nature of being human these days and being connected digitally to all the facets of life from personal to professional. However, that does not mean they do not have a sense of skepticism and concern. While the acceptance may be high in most statistics on the fact that consumers know their data are being collected, the increased heightened sensitivity of feeling secure continues to grow.

The Consumer Concern

The Pew Research Center noted in 2023 that 81 percent of adults are concerned about how companies are collecting data about them. The crux of this concern is the idea that there is not enough transparency in the way of consent or assimilation of that data. So, the first consideration you must make is how good are you at being upfront around the ability to showcase what, where, when, why, and how you are collecting consumer data. Now, let us be honest, even if you have the most well-scripted data privacy policy, not all consumers are going to read it, all the time. The same study from PRC finds that many Americans ignore privacy policies altogether: 56 percent frequently click "agree" without actually reading their content.

So, there is that. You cannot force anyone to read something. However, the fact is you obviously need to ensure your data privacy policy is at least easy to find, accessible, and clear. Clarity is key. This is where at least you can have some level of confidence you can do all you can to ensure an authentic and transparent policy, in the effort to showcase that transparency. Because the other piece as well is the trust consumers have on even understanding the clarity of your policy. PRC also indicated 61 percent think they are ineffective at explaining how companies use people's data.

Crafting a Solid Privacy Policy

Creating a solid data privacy policy is not just about complying with regulations—it is about earning and maintaining consumer trust. A well-crafted policy shows your customers that you respect their data and take their privacy seriously. Here is a guide to help you shape a clear, transparent, and effective data privacy policy for your business.

1. **Be Transparent and Clear**

   Your data privacy policy should be easy to understand. Avoid legal jargon and focus on plain language that informs your users about what data you are collecting, how you are using it, and why. Transparency builds trust, and consumers are more likely to engage with companies they feel are upfront about their practices.

   Best Practice: Break your policy into clear sections with headings like "What Data We Collect," "How We Use Your Data," and "Your Rights." Ensure that users can quickly find the information they need without combing through pages of text.

2. **Define What Data You Collect and Why**

   Be specific about the types of data you collect (e.g., personal information, browsing history, payment details) and provide clear reasons for why you are collecting it. Whether it is to improve services, for marketing, or for legal compliance, transparency around the purpose of data collection is key to gaining user consent.

   Best Practice: Use examples that resonate with your audience. For instance, explain that collecting browsing history helps improve their online experience by personalizing content and recommendations.

3. **Explain How You Protect Data**

Consumers want reassurance that their data are secure. Outline the security measures you have in place, such as encryption, firewalls, and regular audits. While you do not need to give away every technical detail, demonstrating a commitment to robust data security practices can ease concerns.

Best Practice: Include information on how often you update your security protocols and the steps you take to mitigate risks like data breaches.

4. **Ensure Global Compliance**

If your business operates in multiple regions, ensure your policy complies with major privacy laws like the **GDPR (General Data Protection Regulation)** in Europe, **CCPA (California Consumer Privacy Act)**, and other relevant laws such as the **Virginia Consumer Data Protection Act (VCDPA)**. Outline how your company respects these laws and clarify any specific rights that consumers have based on their location.

Best Practice: For companies serving a global audience, consider adding a section that breaks down user rights by region, making it easy for users to understand how their rights differ depending on where they live.

5. **Clarify User Rights**

Users have the right to know what data you hold, to access or correct that data, and in some cases, to request its deletion. Make these rights clear and provide straightforward instructions on how users can exercise them.

Best Practice: Include links or forms that make it easy for users to submit data requests and ensure that your process for responding to these requests is efficient and transparent.

6. **Communicate How You Share Data**

If you share user data with third parties—whether for marketing, partnerships, or operational purposes—make this clear. Consumers are particularly sensitive about who has access to their information, so it is essential to provide detailed information on this point.

Best Practice: Name the categories of third parties you share data with (e.g., payment processors, marketing platforms) and explain the purpose behind each data-sharing activity. Also, include opt-out options for users who prefer not to have their data shared for certain purposes.

7. **Provide Regular Updates**

   Data privacy regulations and best practices are constantly evolving. Make a habit of reviewing and updating your privacy policy regularly to stay compliant and maintain transparency with your users. Any changes should be communicated promptly.

   Best Practice: When you update your policy, notify users directly via e-mail or on your website. A simple message outlining what has changed and why can go a long way in maintaining trust.

8. **Make the Policy Easy to Find**

   Your privacy policy should not be buried in the footer of your website. Make it easily accessible from multiple places on your site, and especially during key interactions where data are collected, like during sign-ups or purchases.

   Best Practice: Include a visible link to your privacy policy on your homepage, in your website's footer, and during checkout or form-submission processes.

By focusing on clarity, transparency, and compliance with global regulations, your data privacy policy can serve as both a legal safeguard and a trust-building tool for your business. Adopting these best practices will help you ensure that your consumers feel secure in their interactions with your brand, which is key to long-term success.

The Consumer Relationship Impact

Cisco (2022) indicated that 81 percent of users believe the way a company treats their personal data is indicative of the way it views them as a customer. The core of that statistic is all about the relationship and how consumers feel they are being treated. Protecting consumer data goes beyond just protecting ourselves internally from lawsuits, brand backlash, and loss in profitability. It is protecting that sacred consumer relationship that many of us work hard to generate.

Now let us be honest, even with the best intent to safeguard our consumer data with modern cybersecurity technologies, elite IT infrastructure, and sound data best practices within our digital teams, things still happen. There is not a 100 percent bullet proof way to prevent cyberattacks, hacking, or data leaks. The point of that though is to evaluate and assume you are doing the best you can through rigorous inspections, testing, and partnership with the IT department to ensure any weak spots of security are uncovered and fixed, if any, at least regularly.

Remember the key aspect of any relationship—even if something goes wrong, it is how you manage the downfall that helps you get yourself back up. When a data breach or an issue with consumer data happens, the most important thing is to be transparent and take steps to rebuild trust. Here is how you can do that:

1. **Own Up to It Quickly**: Do not wait to tell your customers—let them know as soon as possible. They will appreciate the honesty, and delaying only causes more damage. Be upfront about what happened, what data were involved, and how it might affect them.
2. **Take Responsibility**: Avoid pointing fingers or making excuses. Acknowledge the situation and show you are taking charge. Customers need to feel like you are in control and working on a solution.
3. **Lay Out Your Plan**: Let your customers know exactly what you are doing to fix the problem and prevent it from happening again. Offering something like free credit monitoring shows you are serious about protecting their trust.
4. **Keep the Communication Going**: Regular updates are key. Whether through e-mails or social media, make sure your customers know what is happening every step of the way.
5. **Be There for Them**: Make sure your customer service team is ready to help with any questions or concerns. Giving them that individualized touch can go a long way toward rebuilding faith in your brand.

By being open, responsive, and understanding, you can salvage those important customer relationships and show that you are committed to making things right, even in tough situations like data breaches.

Negotiables of Transparency

When a major data breach or misuse of data occurs, transparency is essential to maintaining trust with your digital consumers. But transparency does not mean you have to disclose every technical detail. There is a delicate balance between being open about the breach and protecting the integrity of your internal operations.

Here is the key: **Informing those affected** is nonnegotiable. You need to explain what happened, what data were compromised, and how it impacts them. But while customers want and deserve to know the basics, they do not necessarily need to understand the finer points of your security infrastructure. For example, you might explain that unauthorized access occurred through a vulnerability in your system, but you would not go into detail about specific software weaknesses or the exact steps hackers used to exploit them.

This kind of restraint is important for a few reasons. First, **oversharing technical details can invite further attacks**. If malicious actors learn more about your systems than necessary, they might exploit lingering vulnerabilities that have not yet been patched. It is a bit like giving away the blueprint to your security system while you are still fixing the locks. Instead, focus on letting customers know how you are strengthening your defenses without offering a playbook for potential future breaches.

Second, not every customer wants or needs to know these complexities. Most consumers care about **results and assurances**—what are you doing to make sure it does not happen again, and what actions should they take? They want to feel that you are handling the situation competently without being overwhelmed by jargon or technical explanations they might not fully understand.

This does not mean you are hiding anything. It is about **strategic transparency**—sharing enough to keep customers informed and reassured, but not so much that you inadvertently put your company at greater risk. You can say something like—"We have identified a vulnerability in our system and are working to fix it. Here is what we are doing to protect your data in the future"—without explaining how the specific exploit worked or the exact technology involved.

Let us consider a real-world example: In 2017, Equifax, one of the largest credit reporting agencies, experienced a massive data breach that affected over 147 million people. Initially, their response was slow and unclear, which eroded trust. When they finally addressed the public, they acknowledged the breach but did not get bogged down in the technicalities of how it happened. They informed consumers that personal data had been exposed and outlined a plan for corrective action, including offering free credit monitoring and other services. While the situation was far from ideal, their focus on **providing a clear, consumer-friendly response** rather than overwhelming technical details helped to stabilize some trust in the wake of the breach.

This example highlights the importance of addressing the breach directly but carefully. **Transparency should build confidence** and demonstrate accountability, not expose vulnerabilities, or confuse your audience. By focusing on the steps you are taking to protect consumer data and prevent future breaches, you can maintain trust without compromising the security of your operations.

Bottom Line: Trust

Trust is easily the most important concept when it comes to digital consumer relationships, especially when we are talking about handling and safeguarding customer data. In the digital world, where consumers are constantly sharing personal information—whether it is for shopping, signing up for services, or interacting on social media—trust becomes the foundation of the entire relationship. Without it, everything else falls apart.

Managing customer data is not just about keeping it secure; it is about **showing consumers that we take their privacy seriously** and that we are doing everything in our power to protect them from things like hacking or misuse of their data. Consumers expect the brands they interact with to act ethically, especially when it comes to their sensitive information. And let us be honest, a single breach or data misuse scandal can completely destroy years of trust that took time and effort to build.

When customers trust you with their data, they don't just trust your products or services—they trust your **integrity and commitment to doing the right thing**. They want to know that their personal information will not be mishandled or fall into the wrong hands. This means we must be proactive, not just reactive, when it comes to cybersecurity. It is about **ethical responsibility**—implementing strong data protection measures and constantly evaluating risks to ensure that their trust is well-placed.

But it goes beyond just the technical aspect. It is also about how we communicate. **Transparency plays a huge role here**. If there is a hiccup—like a data breach—we need to be upfront and honest about it. Consumers do not expect perfection, but they do expect accountability. Owning up to mistakes, explaining what is being done to fix them, and ensuring that those mistakes will not happen again are all essential to keeping that trust intact.

In the end, trust is what keeps customers coming back. It is what encourages them to share more data, make more purchases, and recommend your brand to others. If we lose that trust, we lose not just customers but the credibility and reputation of our brand. So, the way we manage and protect customer data is not just about avoiding risk—it is about **fostering long-term relationships** built on a solid foundation of trust.

AI in All This

AI is quickly becoming a crucial asset for protecting consumer data, and digital strategists need to fully understand its role in staying ahead of security threats. The beauty of AI lies in its ability to **analyze massive amounts of data and detect threats in real-time**, something manual systems simply cannot do at the same scale or speed.

Here is a closer look at how AI fits into the picture:

1. **Constant Monitoring**: AI continuously scans your digital environment, detecting unusual patterns like unexpected login locations or strange spikes in data access. It does not wait for a breach to happen—it is on the lookout 24/7, identifying issues before they become major problems.
2. **Real-Time Threat Detection**: By analyzing historical data on cyberattacks, AI can predict and identify new threats based on

behavior patterns. If a hacker attempts to exploit a vulnerability that is like past breaches, AI can step in before any real damage occurs.

3. **Instant Response**: When a threat is detected, AI can act immediately, doing things like blocking suspicious activity, locking compromised accounts, or notifying your security team—all in real-time. This drastically reduces the window of opportunity for attackers.

4. **Learning and Adapting**: AI systems improve over time. The more data they process, the better they get at recognizing threats. This adaptive quality means AI can keep pace with evolving cyberthreats, learning from every breach attempt and continuously strengthening your defense.

For digital strategists, incorporating AI into your security strategy is no longer optional—it is essential. **AI offers a proactive, always-on approach** to data protection, which is crucial for maintaining consumer trust. It keeps your systems secure in the background, freeing your team to focus on higher-level strategy rather than constantly firefighting security issues.

AI allows you to be ahead of the curve—spotting threats, acting, and learning from each incident, all while protecting your customers' data and building trust in your brand.

Key Points

- Building trust with customers means protecting their data and being fair.
- Be honest and open when problems with data happen.
- Customers know their data are used, so clear communication is important.
- Following data privacy laws and caring about customer data build loyalty.
- AI helps keep customer data safe by spotting and stopping threats quickly.

As We Move Ahead

Now that the notion of ensuring trust is intact, you must now absorb the digital consumer decision-making process. What exactly are those steps? Knowing them and how we participate as the digital strategist in that process to influence is critical. We go further now into the digital consumer journey—from consideration to desire. The next chapter focuses on how to optimize the digital experience, to capitalize on this next phase of the digital consumer journey.

CHAPTER 7

Bridging Interest to Desire: Critical Influences

The desire for knowledge, like the thirst of riches, increases ever with the acquisition of it.

—Laurence Sterne

Chapter Overview

This quote speaks to the innate human drive for more—more knowledge, more satisfaction, more fulfillment—echoing the critical moment in the consumer decision-making process known as the desire phase. In this chapter, we will dive into how desire, when properly influenced, can act as the key turning point in the digital consumer's journey from consideration to conversion. Desire is more than a fleeting interest; it is a powerful force that drives action. To understand it fully, we must examine the psychological and emotional triggers that stir it.

Bridging the Consumer Connection

As a digital executive, you are already aware of how crucial it is to understand every step of the consumer journey. One of the most important distinctions you need to focus on is the difference between interest and desire. When a consumer is in the "interest" stage, they are exploring—they are looking at options, comparing products, and gathering information. It is an important phase, but just having their interest is not enough to drive conversions.

Desire, however, is where the real magic happens. This is when a consumer moves from casual curiosity to actual intent. They are emotionally engaged, and now they are ready to make a decision. The key for you is figuring out how to bridge the gap between these two stages. It is not just about providing more information at this point; it is about creating a narrative that makes your product or service irresistible.

Remember, too, that you need to understand that in the desire phase of the digital journey, distinguishing between what consumers want and what they need is critical. Wants are driven by emotions, preferences, and aspirations, while needs are more practical and rooted in solving specific problems. Your strategy should focus on tapping into emotional drivers to create a sense of urgency while simultaneously addressing the consumer's core needs. By aligning your offerings with both, you build stronger connections, increase conversions, and foster long-term loyalty. Recognizing this balance will help position your products more effectively and drive impactful results.

Psychological Influences

At this point in the customer journey, consumers have moved beyond basic awareness and interest—they are now evaluating whether your product or service is worth pursuing. This is where emotions, perceived value, urgency, and social validation come into play. For digital strategists, mastering these psychological drivers can mean the difference between capturing a consumer's attention and converting that desire into a purchase. To effectively move consumers from consideration to decision, it is essential to tap into their emotional and psychological needs.

Emotional Connection

Harvard Business Review (2016) reported that an emotional connection between a customer and the organization is 52 percent more valuable than a highly satisfied customer. When consumers reach the desire phase, it is not just about features or specs anymore—it is about how they feel about your product. This emotional connection is often the difference between someone casually browsing and deciding, "I need this." At this stage, consumers are asking, "How will this product make me feel? Will it elevate my lifestyle, make me feel accomplished, or give me a sense of belonging?" For example, think about why people buy luxury cars. It is not just about transportation; it is about status, pride, and the thrill of owning something exceptional.

How to Apply This

As a digital strategist, you need to build that emotional connection by telling a compelling story. This is where brands like Apple excel. They do not just sell products—they sell a vision of creativity, innovation, and belonging to an exclusive community. You can do the same by crafting messages that speak to your audience's deeper desires. Use storytelling that connects your product to their identity or aspirations. What emotion does your product evoke? Highlight that in your campaigns.

Leverage visuals, music, and language that tap into those emotional triggers, making the consumer feel like they need your product in their life. Emotionally connected consumers are also the strongest advocates. Motista (2018) found that 71 percent of customers recommend a brand based on their emotional connection to it. Therefore, the win in the initial connection to conversion is a significant value; however, the ability to grow demand with referrals and word-of-mouth due to emotional connection is an added value when focusing on these areas.

Perceived Value

During the desire phase, consumers are weighing whether the product is worth their time and money. It is not just about price—it is about perceived value. What are they getting out of the deal? Are the benefits strong enough to justify the purchase? For example, if someone is eyeing a new smartphone, they are not just thinking about the cost; they are considering whether the advanced camera, longer battery life, and sleek design are worth the investment.

How to Apply This

Your job is to show that your product's value far outweighs its cost. Highlight both the rational benefits (like features and performance) and emotional benefits (like how it enhances their lifestyle). Amazon Prime is a notable example—they push their membership's value by emphasizing fast shipping, streaming content, and exclusive deals. They have made Prime feel like a smart investment that offers much more than just delivery services. For your strategy, think about how you can emphasize value across multiple touchpoints—whether that is through pricing models, exclusive offers, or emphasizing the long-term benefits of your product.

Fear of Missing Out (FOMO)

FOMO is a powerful motivator in the desire phase. When people feel like they are going to miss something exclusive or in high demand, they are much more likely to act quickly. The fashion industry, especially brands like Supreme, has mastered this tactic. They create limited-edition drops that spark a sense of urgency and scarcity, making consumers rush to purchase before the product is gone. Approximately 60 percent of consumers admit to making purchases within 24 hours due to FOMO. This sense of urgency often comes from limited-time offers, exclusive deals, or events (Holistic SEO 2023).

How to Apply This

You can use FOMO to your advantage by creating urgency in your campaigns. This could be limited-time discounts, exclusive product launches, or low-stock notifications. For example, include countdown timers on your website or send out e-mails with "Only a few left!" messaging. The goal is to make consumers feel like if they do not act now, they are going to miss out on something special. Incorporating FOMO into your digital strategy can significantly shorten the time between desire and action.

Social Proof

Consumers in the desire phase often look for social proof to validate their decision. They want to know—"Have other people bought this product? Are they happy with it?" Whether it's reading reviews, seeing friends use a product, or watching influencer endorsements, social proof provides the reassurance that helps tip the scale toward a purchase. Brands like

Glossier have built their reputation on this, heavily featuring customer testimonials and user-generated content to show that real people love their products. A staggering 87 percent of consumers would not consider doing business with a brand that has less than a 3-star rating, and 94 percent of consumers rely on ratings when choosing businesses (Popupsmart. com 2023).

How to Apply This

Social proof should be a core part of your strategy. Showcase reviews and testimonials prominently on your product pages. HubSpot (2022) stated that 57 percent of customers visit a business's website after they encounter positive testimonials and reviews. Ensure you have a strong syndicated product or service review partnership with companies that specialize in this area and plug them into your website. Solicit reviews directly with your consumers in a manner of offering incentives or entering a sweepstakes for a prize. For example, you could offer a short weekend opportunity for your online consumers to review a product they recently purchased and let them know by doing so they have a chance to win a US$500 gift card. While it may cost you US$500 in expense for one winner, the payoff to generate potentially dozens if not hundreds of product reviews to further engage and connect with other buying consumers is a tremendous payoff!

Use influencer marketing to demonstrate real-world use and satisfaction. Encourage user-generated content by creating campaigns where customers share their experiences with your product on social media. The more authentic and widespread the feedback, the more confident consumers will feel in their decision to buy. Integrating social proof into your digital touchpoints reinforces trust and credibility, pushing consumers from desire to action.

Cognitive Biases

Cognitive biases are mental shortcuts that affect decision-making, often leading consumers to make choices that deviate from rationality. In the desire phase, these biases can significantly influence how consumers perceive your product and, ultimately, whether they decide to purchase. Recognizing and leveraging cognitive biases in your strategy can create powerful triggers that guide consumers toward action. For example, biases like *anchoring*—where people rely heavily on the first piece of information they encounter—can shape how consumers evaluate the price or features of a product.

The Dunning–Kruger Effect, first introduced by psychologists David Dunning and Justin Kruger in their 1999 paper, is a cognitive bias where individuals with low ability in a specific domain overestimate their competence, while highly skilled individuals may underestimate their relative competence. This effect explains a common misalignment between perceived and actual ability.

In the context of consumer confidence, the Dunning–Kruger Effect suggests that consumers with limited knowledge or understanding of a product or market may express higher confidence in their purchasing decisions than more informed consumers. This overconfidence can lead consumers to make poor choices, believing they understand the product or its implications better than they do. On the other hand, more knowledgeable consumers may express uncertainty, despite their expertise, as they are more aware of the complexities involved.

One common cognitive bias is *loss aversion*, where consumers feel the pain of loss more acutely than the pleasure of gain. This can be strategically used in marketing by emphasizing what consumers stand to lose by not purchasing a product. For instance, if they do not take advantage of a limited-time offer, they might miss significant savings or an exclusive item. Highlighting potential loss can drive urgency and compel consumers to act more quickly.

Another important bias is the *bandwagon effect*, where people tend to follow the actions of others. Consumers are more likely to desire a product if they see others purchasing or endorsing it, which ties directly into social proof. When consumers feel that a product is popular or widely accepted, they are more likely to believe it is worth their time and money. This bias can be amplified by showcasing customer reviews, high ratings, or statements like "Join the thousands who love this product."

How to Apply This

To incorporate cognitive biases into your digital strategy, start by anchoring your pricing or benefits. Show the consumer the most premium option first, so that they anchor their perception of value based on that. If they later choose a lower-priced product, they will feel like they are getting a deal. Additionally, leverage loss aversion by creating urgency through limited-time offers or highlighting potential losses (e.g., "Only a few left at this price!"). Use the bandwagon effect by emphasizing popularity through social proof—testimonials, user-generated content, or showcasing how many customers have already made a purchase.

Cognitive Dissonance

Cognitive dissonance happens when consumers experience conflicting feelings or beliefs, often causing hesitation. In the desire phase, this might occur when a consumer wants a product but hesitates due to concerns like price, quality, or necessity.

As a digital strategist, understanding cognitive dissonance is key to overcoming these hurdles. You need to anticipate where these conflicts arise and address them proactively. For instance, when a consumer hesitates, you can reduce dissonance by reinforcing the product's value through positive reviews, guarantees, or addressing potential concerns up front. This helps build trust, making the consumer feel more confident moving from desire to action.

How to Apply It

- **Anticipate Doubts**: Identify common concerns, such as cost or necessity, and use messaging that directly addresses these issues.
- **Provide Reassurance**: Include testimonials, expert endorsements, or product guarantees to reduce perceived risk. Offering free trials or flexible returns also helps ease concerns.
- **Reinforce Decisions**: Follow up with targeted content that reminds consumers of benefits and creates urgency through exclusive offers or discounts.

- **Simplify Choices**: Break down complex options into straightforward solutions, providing clear information to guide consumers confidently.

By applying these tactics, you reduce cognitive dissonance and smooth the consumer's journey from desire to conversion, ensuring a more positive decision-making process.

Case Study: Netflix Knows

Netflix has an impressive way of understanding its audience by leveraging key psychological triggers, and it is something that executives can learn from. When users face endless choices on the platform, Netflix tackles cognitive dissonance by offering curated recommendations like "Because You Watched" or "Top Picks for You." These subtle nudges ease the anxiety of making a decision, making people feel confident they will enjoy their selection. It is a great lesson in how you can simplify decision-making for your customers, reducing friction and increasing satisfaction.

Another psychological tool Netflix uses effectively is FOMO—the fear of missing out. The "Top 10 in Your Country" feature is genius at tapping into this. It not only shows what's trending but also creates urgency. Consumers do not want to miss what everyone else is watching or talking about. By driving this sense of urgency, Netflix keeps viewers engaged and helps content to spread organically. It is a smart way to use social dynamics to increase engagement.

Social proof plays into this too. Seeing shows or movies in the "Trending Now" or "Top 10" categories sends a subtle message: If others are watching it, it must be worth watching. People feel more secure making a choice that seems validated by the crowd. For any business, this teaches the importance of leveraging what others are doing to help consumers feel reassured about their choices.

But where Netflix truly excels is in creating an emotional connection. They do not just push content—they curate experiences that align with viewers' moods and emotional needs. Whether it is a nostalgic series or a binge-worthy original, Netflix knows how to strike an emotional chord. This kind of deep, personal connection is invaluable for building long-term customer loyalty.

Netflix shows us that by understanding consumer psychology, businesses can reduce decision anxiety, create urgency, tap into social validation, and build emotional bonds—all of which drive not just engagement but loyalty.

Right Time, Right Place, Right Position

Mastering consumer psychology in the desire phase of their journey is a game-changer for any marketer looking to elevate their strategy. Here is why: **Understanding exactly what drives a consumer's emotions, motivations, and thought processes puts you in control of the three key pillars of effective marketing—Right Time, Right Place, and Right Position.**

When you tap into the desire state, you are not just guessing when or where to engage your audience; you **know exactly when they are primed to act.** That is the **Right Time**—the moment their emotional triggers are fired, and they are ready to move from consideration to purchase.

Then comes the **Right Place.** Once you have that psychological insight, you are not just showing up in their lives—you are showing up **where it matters most.** Whether it is on their Instagram feed, in their inbox, or on a product page, you are there when their desire is building.

Finally, the **Right Position.** This is where mastery of consumer psychology truly sets you apart. You are not just throwing a product or service in front of them; you are presenting it in a way that speaks directly to their wants, needs, and, most importantly, their emotions. You are positioning your brand as the solution they did not even know they were craving.

Understanding your consumers at the desire level is not just smart marketing—it is **strategic power.** You are not reacting to their behavior; you are predicting it and guiding them toward a conversion with precision.

How Do You Do It?

Here are some best practices and tactics for mastering consumer psychology in the desire phase, keeping it direct and actionable (Figure 7.1):

- **Leverage Emotional Triggers**: Understand what drives your audience emotionally—whether it is excitement, fear of missing out (FOMO), or aspiration. Build your messaging to tap into these emotions at the peak of their desire.
- **Create Urgency**: Limited-time offers, countdowns, or scarcity tactics can push consumers from desire to action. Make them feel like they need to act now or risk missing out.
- **Use Social Proof**: Show your audience that others like them are already making the decision to buy. Use reviews, testimonials, or case studies to build trust and create validation.
- **Optimize Timing**: Engage with your audience when they are most likely to convert. Use data analytics to understand when your consumers are most active and prime them with content that fuels their desire during those moments.
- **Be Omnipresent**: Make sure your brand shows up across the channels where your consumers are actively searching, shopping, and engaging. Stay on top of mind without being invasive.
- **Tailor Your Offers**: Personalize promotions based on what your consumer has shown interest in. Make it feel like the offer is

Figure 7.1 Desire phase best practices

uniquely crafted for them, which increases the likelihood of them converting.

- **Simplify the Path to Purchase**: Once desire is triggered, do not let friction kill it. Make sure the buying process is smooth, with minimal clicks and easy navigation to complete the purchase.

These practices ensure you are not just meeting consumers where they are but you are also pushing them to act when they are most ready.

Creating Frictionless Digital Experience

Now that you have the acumen to understand the psychological state and influences of your consumer, you know the need to build that frictionless experience for them. From a behavioral perspective, frictionless digital marketing and shopping tap directly into cognitive ease and motivation. Consumers naturally seek the path of least resistance, often making decisions based on how mentally effortless an experience feels. When an online experience is seamless, it reduces cognitive load, making it easier for the consumer to stay engaged and motivated to complete their purchase.

When you create frictionless digital marketing and shopping experiences, you are tapping directly into how the brain naturally works. Consumers are wired to seek the easiest, most effortless path, so when you give them a seamless journey—from browsing to checkout—you are keeping them engaged and motivated.

Establishing the Framework

- **Cognitive Ease Matters**: When your site is easy to navigate, with clear layouts and quick loading times, consumers process it without much mental effort. That ease feels good. They are more likely to stay, complete their purchase, and leave with a positive view of your brand.
- **Conditioned for Convenience**: Today's consumers expect convenience—one-click purchases, fast pages, personalized recommendations. You have likely seen it: When everything flows smoothly, they are happy and keep coming back. But the

moment you throw in roadblocks—slow pages, complicated checkouts—you risk losing them to frustration.

- **Simplify Choices**: Too many options can overwhelm a customer, causing decision paralysis. You can avoid that by designing a choice structure that's clear and limits irrelevant options. When you guide them efficiently, they will make decisions faster, and you will see higher conversion rates.
- **Emotions Drive Actions**: Friction creates negative emotions like anxiety or frustration. Whether it is an overly complicated checkout or hidden fees, those pain points drive people away. If they feel in control and reassured, they will complete the purchase.
- **Set the Right Expectations**: Every smooth experience you offer sets a standard. When you consistently meet or exceed that, consumers expect it every time. But if you add new friction—maybe a confusing update or unexpected hurdle—you are breaking their trust, and they might not come back.

Key Tactics

Creating a frictionless digital experience is all about removing barriers between your customers and their desired actions. Here is how you can ensure your digital platforms keep consumers engaged and coming back.

Speed Is Key: Your consumers demand instant results. According to research, 53 percent of mobile users will abandon a page if it takes more than 3 seconds to load. To keep them engaged, you need to prioritize fast-loading pages. This means optimizing images, leveraging caching, and minimizing scripts to ensure smooth performance across all devices. If your site is slow, you are likely losing a significant portion of potential customers before they even see your offerings (Google, 2016).

Simplified Navigation: Consumers value simplicity, and 76 percent say that the ease of finding information is the most key factor in a website's design. If users cannot quickly locate what they are looking for, frustration sets in, leading to high bounce rates. You can improve navigation by using clear, intuitive menus, a strong search function, and reducing clutter on your site. It is about guiding the user, not overwhelming them with options (Hubspot, 2017).

One-Click Purchasing: Amazon's success with one-click purchasing has set the gold standard for seamless transactions. Reducing the number of steps in your checkout process can dramatically reduce cart abandonment, which averages around 69.57 percent. This means enabling features like guest checkout and auto-fill for payment details to make it as effortless as possible for users to complete a purchase. Simplify, and watch conversions rise (Popupsmart).

Mobile Optimization: With over 56 percent of Internet traffic coming from mobile, optimizing your website for mobile use is nonnegotiable. Consumers expect a flawless experience on their phones and 57 percent will not recommend a business if their mobile experience is poor. Responsive design, fast load times, and easy navigation on mobile devices are essential to reduce friction and keep your audience engaged, no matter what device they use (Firework, 2026).

Payment Flexibility: Today's consumers want options when it comes to payments. In fact, 63% prefer multiple payment methods at checkout, including digital wallets and buy-now-pay-later services. Offering flexibility not only enhances the customer experience but also reduces the likelihood of abandoned carts. Providing diverse, secure payment options helps streamline the final step of the buying process (Exploding Topics, 2025).

By focusing on these key areas—speed, navigation, one-click purchasing, mobile optimization, and payment flexibility—you will create a smoother, more engaging digital experience that reduces friction and drives better results for your business. By focusing on these behavioral factors, you are not just removing obstacles—you are designing experiences that align with how people think and act. This is what leads to higher conversions and lasting customer loyalty.

Neuromarketing

Neuromarketing is your secret weapon to unlocking the emotional and psychological drivers behind consumer decisions. It is not just about data; it is about diving deep into what truly *moves* people. By studying brain activity, eye movement, and even heart rates, neuromarketing reveals what *really* catches attention and drives action. In the 2020s, with competition fiercer than ever, you need more than just surface-level insights. **You need to tap into emotions** that compel consumers to engage and buy.

According to Martin Lindstrom (2010), author of *Buyology*, "Our brain makes decisions on an emotional level up to 80 percent of the time." This is why **you need to prioritize emotional connections** over just delivering information. Neuromarketing's core lies in how the brain reacts to sensory inputs—visual design, product placement, or even packaging color—all of which trigger emotional responses. Understanding these can help you create campaigns that do not just inform but truly **connect** with your audience, shaping their perception and influencing their final decisions.

How You Can Use Neuromarketing

- **Sensory Engagement:** You can analyze how different images, sounds, or designs generate positive emotional reactions. It is not about guessing; it is about knowing which sensory cues work best.
- **Emotional Measurement:** Use tools like fMRI, EEG, or biometric data to see how your audience feels in real-time. This helps you craft messages that resonate deeply with their subconscious desires.
- **Cognitive Triggers:** Take advantage of powerful triggers like scarcity, social proof, or FOMO to push consumers toward action. **These emotional levers** make the difference between consideration and conversion.
- **Behavioral Insights:** You can predict consumer behavior by understanding how emotions drive decisions. Eye-tracking and brainwave analysis show you what is working and where friction exists in your digital experiences.

How to Apply Neuromarketing Right Now

Incorporate neuromarketing into every phase of your consumer's journey. When consumers are in the desire phase, **you need to hit them with emotionally evocative content**—from video storytelling to personalized messaging that speaks to their subconscious. **Design your digital experiences** to anticipate and address their emotions at every touchpoint, whether it is on your website, in e-mail marketing, or through social media.

By using neuromarketing, **you can eliminate friction** and create a seamless, emotionally satisfying experience that not only grabs attention but also builds trust and loyalty. As this field continues to evolve, **you will have a more scientific edge** in creating high-impact, emotionally resonant campaigns that deeply connect with your audience.

In short, neuromarketing takes you from being just data-driven to **emotion-driven**, making the consumer's emotional experience the heart of your strategy. As neuromarketing expert Roger Dooley (2012) puts it, "You can't always trust what consumers say, but **you can trust their brain responses**."

Case Study: Coca-Cola's Neuromarketing in Action

In recent years, **Coca-Cola** has successfully used neuromarketing to connect with digital consumers on a deeper, emotional level through its famous "Share a Coke" campaign. This initiative involved replacing the Coca-Cola logo with popular first names, turning a simple soda into a personalized experience. The strategy, rooted in neuromarketing principles, was designed to tap into the human need for recognition and personal connection. Coca-Cola employed neuromarketing techniques like **EEG** and **eye-tracking** to understand consumer reactions to the packaging, gauging their emotional and cognitive responses to various designs and ad concepts.

By personalizing the experience and involving consumers in a new, exciting way, Coca-Cola was able to generate a significant emotional response. This connection not only made consumers feel more involved but also prompted them to share their experiences on social media, turning the campaign into a viral sensation. The campaign sparked massive consumer engagement as people posted images of their personalized Coke bottles on social media platforms, tagging friends, and further amplifying the brand's reach.

The "Share a Coke" campaign's success demonstrates the power of neuromarketing in digital consumer engagement. By appealing to consumers' emotional triggers—such as recognition, nostalgia, and social connection—Coca-Cola effectively strengthened brand loyalty. This is a prime example of how a brand can leverage neuromarketing to build a more profound connection with its audience in the digital age.

AI in All This

AI gives you the power to dive deep into consumer psychology, offering insights that surpass traditional approaches. By combining advanced analysis with precise technology execution and neuroscience, you can uncover what truly drives consumer behavior. It is not just about tracking surface-level actions; AI enables you to anticipate customer needs and desires by understanding the underlying emotions and cognitive triggers that influence their decisions.

This means you can move beyond general strategies and create personalized, emotionally resonant experiences that speak directly to your audience's subconscious. AI's ability to analyze vast amounts of data in real-time allows you to identify patterns, predict behavior, and adapt your approach quickly. Whether it is through personalized messaging, targeted ads, or optimized user experiences, AI gives you the tools to make smarter, more informed decisions.

Neuroscience adds another layer, allowing you to understand how sensory inputs, like design or product placement, trigger emotional responses. By leveraging this understanding, you can craft campaigns that connect on a deeper, psychological level, ensuring your strategies are not just seen but are also felt. This capability is crucial in building stronger customer relationships, increasing loyalty, and driving conversions.

Key Points

- Create a story that makes your product feel essential to move consumers from interest to desire.
- Focus on emotional connections by aligning your product with what consumers aspire to.
- Show benefits and create urgency with limited-time offers to encourage purchases.
- Use reviews and tactics like FOMO to push consumers to act.
- Tap into emotional triggers with neuromarketing to connect with consumers on a deeper level.

As We Move Ahead

Feeling emotional yet? Hopefully, it is not that, but the feeling of empowerment! You can now understand that the emotional connections built with your consumers with keen assessment of psychological influences will strengthen your strategic toolbox. Now, you are thinking, how do I take all of this newfound appreciation for this knowledge and start executing it with sound digital tactics and strategies? Well, in the next chapter we are going to dive into the ins-and-outs of one of the most important strategies in digital marketing—personalization. It will be taking the desire phase to a higher level, taking the learnings from the psychologies and emotions of our consumers, and building that 1:1 engagement they so deserve.

CHAPTER 8

Personalization and Customer Journeys: AI-Fueled Experiences

People will forget what you said, people will forget what you did, but people will never forget how you made them feel.
—Maya Angelou

Chapter Overview

Maya Angelou's quote perfectly captures the essence of personalization discussed in this chapter: While consumers may forget the specific details of a campaign or the products offered, they will always remember the feeling of being understood and valued. Personalization is about creating meaningful, emotionally engaging experiences that resonate on an individual level. So, with this chapter, let's get personal.

First, What Are You Waiting For?

If you don't have a form of personalization up and running, you are not doing true customer-centric digital marketing. End of story.

Before diving into personalization and journey-building strategies, it's crucial to establish a baseline: Personalization is not a luxury; it's an expectation. Today's consumers expect brands to understand them—not just broadly but also at an individual level. McKinsey & Company (2023) stated that "according to a McKinsey & Company survey, 71 percent of consumers expect personalized interactions from brands. When these expectations aren't met, 76 percent of consumers feel frustrated and may switch brands." They want relevant experiences, timely communication, and solutions that cater directly to their needs and preferences. Without personalization, your marketing is missing the mark, failing to connect on a human level that today's competitive digital landscape demands.

Personalization is the core connection to acquisition but, ultimately, loyalty and retention. The average consumer has more choices than ever before and fewer and fewer opportunities to judge their quality in advance. They're increasingly expecting the brands they engage with online to understand who they are and to offer interactions that are both effortless and relevant. It's not enough to know your audience—you need to know them well enough to meet them where they are in their buying journey and with an awareness of exactly what they're looking for.

The task of personalizing experiences isn't just a missed opportunity: it's a strategic mistake to leave yourself behind your competitors who have better understood that a soul-less sales message will never win a customer-centric digital marketing war. It's personalization that turns digital marketing into a dialogue, not a broadcast. It's what turns a random online person into a unique individual: With personalization your customers become real and more so as you keep collecting more data about them. So, whether we talk about advanced personalization or journey-building, bear in mind: If you haven't started doing any personalization yet, it's simply not customer-centric digital marketing you're doing.

Stop Making Excuses

Trust me, I have seen it firsthand though—the skepticism, or possibly confusion, from internal stakeholders wondering about why even bother about investing in personalization technology. Even the largest of retailers in the world have struggled even after the pandemic to understand the core needs of personalization and putting it on the bottom of the IT roadmap. Now, is it easy to conduct personalization? Well, implementing, it should be if you have the right personalization software partner. However, let's not even discuss them yet and that relationship. We will get to that.

The first question—are there any potentially legitimate reasons as to why your company has not started personalization yet? It could truly be a cost dynamic. Maybe it's a resource constraint on getting the technical acumen to build it. Perhaps it's the ability you don't have the aptitude for or you don't have someone on the team to manage it full time, because it is a full-time commitment. Some of these are valid, in theory. This is where we go back to the evaluation and ROI of such technology and perhaps an agency doing it for you.

However, ask yourself, is your lack of conducting personalization is based on legitimate reasons or just risk-averse excuses? If the latter, let's dive into that.

Now, within the following stats, some of these companies, and companies in general, may have some form of personalization that is rudimentary or they may have none at all. Moreover, just like any technology, it's not about "just having it" on autopilot either. More on that soon. Here are some common statistics companies have concerning personalization, with suggestions to consider combatting those concerns:

- **Managing Unstructured Data**: 95 percent of businesses struggle with unstructured data, which makes up most of the data they generate. These data are harder to analyze but crucial for understanding market trends (Edge Delta 2024).
  1. *Suggestion to Consider*: Use tools that help organize unstructured data automatically, making it easier to sort and analyze.
- **Data Privacy Concerns**: 34 percent of companies have issues protecting data privacy, and many also struggle with data accuracy and processing (Dun and Bradstreet 2022).
  1. *Suggestion to Consider*: Implement clear data privacy rules and tools to make sure data are accurate and handled correctly.
- **Data Literacy and Skills Gap**: 54 percent of Chief Data Officers say their team lacks the skills needed to use data effectively (Edge Delta 2024).
  1. *Suggestion to Consider*: Offer training programs to improve data skills across the team, ensuring everyone can work with data confidently.
- **Scalability Issues**: Many companies don't plan for how their data systems will grow, which makes it hard to keep analyzing data effectively (3Pillar 2022).
  1. *Suggestion to Consider*: Choose flexible systems that can grow as your data grow, to keep up with your increasing needs.

- **Cloud Computing Limitations**: 54 percent of companies are using cloud computing for data analytics, but it often struggles with real-time processing (Edge Delta 2022).
  1. *Suggestion to Consider*: Use both cloud and local systems (edge computing) to handle real-time data better and make faster decisions.

While a lot of these stats focus on data challenges, like managing unstructured data or scaling analytics, there's more to the story. It's not just about the tools or technology; it's also about the mindset and culture within the company. Without a culture that truly values data and a strategic approach to making decisions based on it, even the best tools won't make a difference. This goes back to what we talked about in Chapter 2, where the importance of creating a data-driven customer-centric culture is highlighted. So, if your company is struggling with cultural barriers or strategic alignment, revisit Chapter 2 for guidance and then come back here to apply those principles to the technical and methodology side.

The point is, stop making excuses. There is always an avenue of resources, training, technology, or a build to investment to get to a point to either start conducting personalization or optimizing it.

AI-Driven Techniques to Tailored Experiences

The reality is that consumers today not only tolerate personalization but in fact expect it—AI has elevated personalization from the icing on the cake, as it were, to the minimum expectation. When you make a consumer feel like your brand truly understands who they are, you're doing more than winning a sale—you're making a friend. And if anything, the secret to doing that effectively is—AI.

Whether you are looking at increasing conversions or cultivating your relationships with your customers, AI allows you to create experiences tailored to each user. Let's dive into some of the most effective techniques, best practices, and considerations when leveraging AI to optimize your personalization.

Predictive Analytics and Personalized Recommendations

Picture the customer on your site: Every click, every page they stay on, is a clue as to what they might want next. Hub-and-spoke is the domain of AI-informed predictive analytics, which both Netflix and Amazon use to great success. Netflix "knows" what you watched before because it used AI to figure out what you'll watch next. This is how Netflix suggests titles to watch. Amazon is a master at this too: It "knows" what you bought, because it used AI to predict what you'd purchase next.

The secret for practitioners is to keep those algorithms learning. Algorithms such as collaborative filtering and content-based filtering are great tools, if used correctly, but they need to be fed fresh data to keep the engines running. The worst possible time to recommend someone a book is when it's been so long since their purchase that the recommendations seem stale and out-of-date—just the kind of awkward moment that can turn anyone off your site. If you want to avoid this, make sure you use a hybrid model—follow best practices and mix and match your approaches, as this can make your suggestions feel much more precise.

Dynamic Content Personalization

Personalization is not just about the product; it is about the experience. AI can pull pages together and adjust the content on the fly for each user. A first-time buyer might see discounts or popular items upon arrival to the homepage, whereas a repeat user might see pages based on prior searches.

The secret sauce? Natural Language Processing (NLP)—it is possible to gauge sentiment from previous interactions to understand a user's mood. If a user had an issue the last time they used the product, perhaps make support options more visible on the next visit. Just don't go too far—customers might not react well if an interaction feels too invasive. Always err on the side of caution. Be upfront and explicit with your users as to how you are using their data and give them the ability to make changes to their privacy settings.

Chatbots and Conversational AI

Have you ever spoken to a chatbot and felt like it almost wasn't a bot at all? That's conversational AI. And it's an effective way to scale individual interactions. Whether responding to queries about products, helping a customer through the purchase process, or handling post-purchase inquiries, chatbots make it all feel personal.

And to get that right, your chatbots have to be trained well: They must be able to answer all sorts of queries, not just product questions, to seem genuinely helpful, and they've got to be really good at sentiment analysis. A good chatbot will understand when a customer is angry and will change its tone—empathize instead of pitch.

Hyper-Personalized E-mail Campaigns

Generic e-mail blasts? Sometimes, ok, but all the time or majority of the time, sorry no. That is a 2005, *maybe* 2010 strategy. In the 2020s, AI starts to help us transition into hyper-personalized e-mails, where every message is based on what you want—from products you'd like to try to the most compelling content to read to the perfect time of day to contact you.

One best practice here is to segment your audience based on behaviors—that is, if one person clicked on a link but another did not, or if one browsed certain pages more than another, and so on—and then to tailor each message accordingly. The cool part is that you can conduct A/B testing all the time, for various elements of your message such as subject line and offer.

Personalized Search Results

Use AI to create a unique set of results for each user of the site. Those rankings are based on the individual's previous behavior—what they've seen or bought before. Even an auto-suggest feature that kicks in when a user begins to type a search query can be personalized—by showing the specific results that are most likely to appeal to the individual at that time.

When trying to implement this, NLP-powered search engines are a must. They do not just deliver results that match the keywords; they understand the user's intentions. This makes the process more intuitive, and the answers given more precise, thus minimizing the friction between the step and the goal.

Adaptive User Interfaces (AUI)

Imagine an interface that runs not just in one way but in as many ways as needed—an interface that is tailored to the individual visitor. A typical Adaptive User Interface (AUI) reflects the fact that different security levels might require a slightly different experience. A frequent visitor gets short-cuts to her saved items, whereas a new visitor is guided through a series of steps. The basic design is the same, but the experience is tailored to meet users where they are—every time.

This means that, in practice, we're going to use AI to recognize user typologies and to properly adapt the interface. AUI can deliver greater engagement, but then testing is everything. The experience needs to flow seamlessly between devices to avoid disorientating the user.

AI-Driven A/B Testing

And while that's all pretty heavy, AI can test things a lot faster and in a lot more granular way. You might test four versions of a page overall, but on every one of those page views, the AI is testing variations with different user segments. It's constant, dynamic.

A best practice? Conduct an A/B test alongside predictive analysis—AI models anticipate user behavior and tests only those alternatives to which AI is most likely to predict higher levels of user interaction to improve the user experience.

AI Is Good and All, but Still

Even if AI gives us the ability to create the most precise and effective tools for personalization, we should remember three crucial points.

- **Data:** Who sees what? Be transparent—explain what data you're collecting and give users control over that data. Comply with privacy laws, including the EU's GDPR and the California Consumer Privacy Act (CCPA).

- **Steering Clear of Over-Personalization**: It's a fine line between the helpful type of personalization and the creepy. Strike the right balance—use AI to help users, not spy on them.
- **Scalability:** if you scale your user base, your personalization must too. Build infrastructure able to grow with you, such as cloud-based solutions.
- **Human Oversight:** Oversight by human beings is required to correct mistakes and prevent blunders. AI is powerful but not foolproof. In fact, I have preached the following statement for several years now, hoping of course for citations in the future, but that's just a personal goal.

Artificial intelligence does not replace human intelligence, it augments human innovation

Personalizing digital experiences with AI is about making users feel like they are being uniquely understood—whether that's through predictive recommendations, composing personalized content, or presenting adaptive user interfaces. Make it so users get the right things at the right time. Just remember to do it respectfully, enhancing what already works but not overpowering users—let them have their privacy and space.

User Profiling

User profiling is the process of collecting and analyzing data about an individual and building a profile to describe their behavior, preferences, interests, and needs. It helps marketers create a digital fingerprint of the users by understanding their needs and preferences, and providing them with tailored experiences, as per their requirements.

How User Profiling Works

User profiling begins with data gathering, where every interaction of a user is tracked—for example, clicks, page views, searches, purchases, time spent on pages, and so on. It is collected by means of tools often embedded in websites, apps, or on social media (e.g., cookies, a tracking code, or data lease) and can then be combined in so-called Customer Data Platforms (CDPs).

Data are collected, and AI and machine learning algorithms process and analyze that data, creating a user profile based on what it uncovers about patterns and preferences. User segments are developed, helping marketers to align content, offers, or experiences with what users may want or expect.

For example, if a user viewed a product page for hiking gear on the website a number of times, the profile would ascribe it an "outdoors aficionado" label, allowing us to later display content to this user—ranging from shoe recommendations to related blog articles—across all touchpoints.

Digital Consumer Journey

The **Digital Customer Journey (DCJ)** represents the path a consumer follows from recognizing a need to acquiring a solution through a product or service. This journey involves five key phases: **awareness, consideration, purchase, retention,** and **advocacy**. Each phase includes various **touchpoints**—moments of interaction between the consumer and the brand—that ultimately determine whether the consumer proceeds to purchase or moves on.

A **user journey map** is crucial for visualizing these interactions and understanding the full scope of the customer experience. Every customer's journey is unique, shaped by individual behaviors and preferences, which means each relationship with these touchpoints will vary.

The DCJ isn't just descriptive; it's a strategic tool for **optimizing customer experience** to enhance sales opportunities and customer satisfaction. In today's market, **customer experience** has become the key brand differentiator, surpassing price and product. A successful strategy requires a seamless integration of all communication channels, ensuring every interaction adds value.

Consumers are increasingly **informed, hyper-connected, and emotionally driven**, and they expect a smooth, engaging experience.

Optimizing the DCJ is essential because the process a customer experiences is just as critical as the purchase itself—without a positive journey, the purchase is unlikely to happen.

Optimizing with Marketing Automation

A marketing automation is all about creating and orchestrating every aspect of **consumer experience**—from the moment they first encounter you to the moment they become your most loyal fan—**personalizing at scale**.

It all begins with the **consumer journey map**. You define the major milestones—**awareness, consideration, purchase, and post-purchase**—and every crucial moment in between. In tools such as HubSpot or Salesforce, you define **workflows** that allow for automations based on user behavior and engagement.

Here's How It Works in Action

- **Lead Generation and Nurturing**: A prospect visits your site or downloads an eBook. Your marketing automation software puts their details in the CRM database, which follows up with an **e-mail autoresponder sequence** that might include more educational content aligned with their interests or challenges, nudging the prospect toward a purchase.
- **Personalization and Targeting**: As the system gathers data, it can "bucket" consumers into similar groups based on their behavior (e.g., opening an e-mail, clicking a link, or making a purchase). Instead of blasting a "shotgun" campaign to everyone, you can now send a highly targeted campaign—**personalized content** relevant to their specific interests.
- **Behavioral Triggers**: A consumer abandons a shopping cart or likes your social post. The automation platform springs into action with a preplanned response—such as a follow-up e-mail with a special offer or a product recommendation based on their browsing history. It's like being in a conversation.

- **Automated Campaigns Across Channels**: Automation doesn't stop at e-mail. It can deliver the right message at the right time across channels—**SMS, social media, ads**, you name it. This consistency helps guide consumers along their journey.
- **Measure and Optimize**: Every step is tracked—who clicked what, which content worked, where the leaks occurred. With all this information, you continually **optimize the journey**, tweaking workflows and finding the sweet spots that increase conversions and enhance the experience.

At its best, **marketing automation** is like a clever, trusty sidekick, maximizing every interaction to bring the consumer a step closer to conversion while nurturing a deep relationship with your company. It's about meeting them where they are and guiding them where you want them to go, one automated step at a time.

Fictional Use Case Example

Background

To improve conversion rates and ramp up retention by building stronger consumer loyalty, Fitness Brand XYZ chose to implement a wide-ranging marketing automation strategy to connect with prospects on as many channels as possible and guide them from awareness to zealous spokes-consumers.

1. **Lead Generation and Nurturing**
   Use Case
   A consumer named Sarah sees an ad for the eBook *"The Ultimate Guide to Home Fitness"* on Instagram by Fitness Brand XYZ. After clicking the ad, she completes a short form to get the eBook for free.
   Automation
   The Fitness Brand XYZ marketing automation tool adds Sarah's information to their CRM database and triggers the start of an e-mail nurturing drip-feed. Over the next 2 weeks, various workout tips and motivational success stories reach Sarah's inbox, each suggesting that the website might have a fitness item that suits her.

2. **Personalization and Targeting**

Use Case

As Sarah interacts with the e-mails, Fitness Brand XYZ's marketing automation tool collects data: She opens most of the e-mails and clicks on links related to yoga apparel.

Automation

The system segments Sarah into a yoga-related target audience. Rather than broadcasting generic campaigns, Fitness Brand XYZ sends her an e-mail with content tailored to her interests (a line of yoga apparel), alongside a discount code for first-time buyers. Personalized content engages Sarah in ways that a generic campaign couldn't, making her more likely to shop.

3. **Behavioral Triggers**

Use Case

Sarah lands on the Fitness Brand XYZ website, adds a yoga mat and a pair of leggings to her virtual shopping cart, and then leaves without buying anything.

Automation

The marketing automation software detects the abandoned cart and sends Sarah an e-mail the following day with information on the items and a 10 percent discount if purchases are completed within 24 hours. It also includes positive reviews of the items from other consumers to provide social proof and encourage the purchase.

4. **Automated Campaigns Across Channels**

Use Case

Sarah completed the purchase, but Fitness Brand XYZ has not interacted with her since. To continue engaging Sarah, Fitness Brand XYZ uses cross-channel automation.

Automation

Sarah is texted a thank-you SMS and invited to join Fitness Brand XYZ's loyalty program. She also sees retargeted Facebook ads promoting new products relevant to her purchase (e.g., yoga blocks and water bottles). The sustained activation across channels keeps Fitness Brand XYZ top of mind.

5. **Measure and Optimize**
   Use Case
   Fitness Brand XYZ wants to refine their marketing approach based on consumer interactions.
   Automation
   Every click, the time Sarah spent on the website, when she opened her e-mails, and when she completed her purchase, all were tracked by the platform. Fitness Brand XYZ learned that abandoned cart e-mails prompted consumers to buy when combined with a discount incentive. They also noticed that Sarah clicked on links to eco-friendly materials, prompting them to tweak future campaigns to target similar consumers with information about their green products.
   Outcome
   Marketing automation allowed Fitness Brand XYZ to guide Sarah from initial awareness to a loyal consumer. Personalized nurturing, behavior-based triggers, consistent cross-channel engagement, and continual optimization provided a frictionless, enjoyable consumer experience that ended in conversion, ultimately creating a brand advocate in Sarah.

Overcoming Challenges

Regarding personalization, every business grapples with the same issues or barriers to entry, and to be successful you'll need to find your way through them. So let's examine a few of the most common personalization hurdles and discuss how you, as an executive, can lead your organization in overcoming them.

1. **Data Silos: The Personalization Blocker**
   The most visible challenge in personalization is **data silos**. When your consumer data are stored in myriad "data lakes" throughout your organization, it can be very difficult to get a single view of the consumer journey. Personalization depends on having a clear understanding of your consumer, but, if your data sources are not

talking to each other, then you're trying to put a puzzle together with missing pieces.

Solution: Break through these silos by using **integrated technology** and establishing a culture of **collaboration**. Investing in a centralized data platform, such as a customer data platform (CDP), can help unify data sources and provide your teams with a holistic view of each consumer. Equally important is setting up a structure for **cross-functional communication**. Personalization is not a job for the marketing department only; it's a company-wide effort. Make sure your teams are on the same page and that you're allowing them to share consumer data freely.

2. **Technology Limitations: The Roadblock**

The second challenge is **technology barriers** that might exist, whether it's a legacy system that doesn't integrate well with your new personalization software, or an absence of technology capable of processing high volumes of consumer data in real-time. If you have outdated technology, it will limit your capacity to deliver the personalized experience that resonates with today's consumers.

Solution: Make technology an **enabler**, rather than a bottle-neck. Take stock of your current tech stack and then invest in the right tools for what you're trying to achieve. This can mean adding **marketing automation** and **AI-driven modules** to your CRM system or investing in new platforms capable of integrating with your systems to process large datasets. This doesn't have to mean a major overhaul. Sometimes, **incremental changes** help—such as adding integration layers or new modules to your systems without breaking the bank.

3. **Resource Constraints: The People Problem**

There's also the issue of **budget and people**. Personalization requires content, data mining, technology, and people to run it, and, for many companies, especially those that are scaling up, talent and cost can be an issue.

Solution: Build from the bottom up, **prioritizing high-impact areas**. First, don't wait to have a mature personalization technology infrastructure. Prioritizing your most valuable consumers—the ones who generate the most value for the business—is an easy first step for any company. **Automation** can also help in developing and scaling personalized experiences. If your skillset is too thin, consider outsourcing components of personalization, such as content creation or data analysis. Remember that personalization is a journey—taking small steps that allow you to demonstrate success and unlock more spending and resources over time is the best way to go.

4. **Over-Personalization and Consumer Fatigue: The Fine Line**
A less obvious, but no less crucial challenge is the risk of **over-personalization**. Even as you strive to provide increasingly personalized experiences, there is a danger of overkill, which could backfire—alienating the consumer or even provoking privacy concerns. Picture receiving too many e-mails that make it feel like the brand knows you a little too well: from impressive to creepy, pretty quick.

   Solution: **Strike a balance**. Too much personalization alienates, but if it feels helpful rather than intrusive, you're on the right track. Use consumer data responsibly and be transparent about how you use it. Give consumers choices—regularly ask whether they'd prefer more or less contact and the type of content they receive. To avoid overload, use **segmentation** wisely. Don't send every consumer every offer; make sure offers are targeted to segments that have expressed interest. **A/B testing** helps too—test your personalized campaigns, see how consumers react, and adjust accordingly.

Building a Sustainable Personalization Strategy

The downside of personalization is that it involves a winding road. As an executive, your job is making sure the base of the triangle—**integration, technology, and resourcing**—is as strong as possible to carry you and your team on this journey.

- **Break Down Data Silos**: We operate in a data-driven world. To create a truly personalized experience, you need a unified repository of data about your consumer.
- **Invest in Technology**: The real value in personalization comes from your investment in technology that controls how you interact with your consumer.

- **Be Strategic on Resourcing and Optimize Spend**: Don't make the mistake of investing in technology and people without considering what you truly need to spend.
- **Identify the Line between Personalization and Privacy**: The most complex challenge is mastering the line between personalization and privacy.
- **Stay Nimble and Ahead of the Game**: Now that you are aware of the challenges and opportunities of personalization, you should revisit your business strategy if personalization hasn't made it to your agenda yet.

Key Points

- Personalization is essential for meeting consumer expectations in today's market.
- AI-driven personalization, like predictive analytics, enhances consumer engagement.
- Overcoming challenges requires addressing data silos, technology limitations, and resource constraints.
- Avoid over-personalization to prevent consumer fatigue and privacy concerns.
- Personalization efforts must be supported by cross-departmental collaboration and effective tools.

As We Move Ahead

As we move ahead, it's clear that personalization is a vital part of any digital strategy, offering tailored experiences that resonate with consumers. However, personalization alone can sometimes fall short of converting interest into action, which is why incorporating Conversion Rate Optimization (CRO) is crucial. CRO helps to identify and address the points where consumers stall in their journey, ensuring that personalized efforts effectively lead to closed deals and increased sales. Combining personalization with CRO ensures a seamless consumer experience that maximizes conversions and builds lasting loyalty. The next chapter will dive into this.

CHAPTER 9

Closing the Deal: Conversion Rate Optimization

Measure what is measurable and make measurable what is not so.
—Galileo Galilei

Chapter Overview

It might not be that Galileo had conversion rate optimization in mind, specifically, but the point remains. In the aspect of conversion rate optimization, everything from call-to-action button color to form length is fair game for measurement, testing, and optimization. If you're not measuring it, how do you know it needs to be optimized? This chapter takes you through the science of creating gold out of figures: taking those small, worthy, measurable tweaks and turning them into conversion gold.

Convert Rate Optimization

Alright, let's talk about **Conversion Rate Optimization** or CRO for short. If you've ever wondered how to get more people to take the desired action on your website—whether it's making a purchase, signing up for a newsletter, or booking a demo—CRO is the strategy you need to focus on. In simple terms, CRO is all about enhancing your website or landing pages to boost the percentage of visitors who convert. It's about taking what you already have, like your website traffic, and making sure as many of those people as possible are actually doing what you want them to do.

Rather than think of this as an abstract concept, think of your website the way you would a retail store—people enter, browse, and you want to get them to leave with something in their proverbial shopping cart. CRO allows you to figure out what's causing people to "get stuck" in the digital store, why they're leaving with things, and how to improve the experience so that they'll more successfully buy, click, or subscribe.

Best Practices

Now, if you're looking to improve conversions on your site, here are some best practices that have been proven to work:

1. **Reduce Friction**
   One of the biggest reasons visitors don't convert is the presence of friction—anything within your site that prevents consumers from doing what you want them to do. This could be slow loading times, a confusing navigation bar, or too many steps in the checkout process. Your goal should be to make it as easy as possible for visitors to take action. Make forms shorter, remove distractions, and streamline or eliminate multistep processes.

2. **Leverage Social Proof**
   Digital consumers are influenced by the actions of those around them, which is where social proof comes into play. Incorporate customer reviews, testimonials, and trust badges to enhance credibility. When visitors see others' positive experiences, they are more likely to trust your brand and be inspired to convert.

3. **Optimize CTAs**
   The call to action (CTA) is the most important element on your page. Make sure it's clear, visible, and tells visitors exactly what they will get when they click on it, such as "Get Started Now" or "Claim Your Free Trial." Experiment with the color, location, and phrasing to see what resonates best with your audience.

4. **Personalize the Experience**
   Modern digital consumers expect some level of personalization when visiting your website. If you know who the visitor is (e.g., they've visited before or abandoned a cart), use that information to create a more connected experience for them. Personalized content, offers, and reminders can make a huge difference in convincing someone to convert.

5. **Reduce Anxiety**

Consumers can often feel anxious about buying online—they may worry about the security of their credit card information or making the wrong choice. Address these concerns directly. Add guarantees, post your pricing prominently, and provide instant help options like live chat. If you think your visitor is hesitant to buy, addressing these fears will pay off.

6. **Use Visual Cues**

We navigate the world primarily through sight, so visual cues like arrows, contrasting colors, and whitespace should be used to guide the viewer's attention. For example, if you want to highlight the "Buy Now" button on your landing page, use color contrast to make it stand out, increasing the likelihood of clicks.

7. **Optimize for Mobile**

This one is critical for optimizing because mobile is no longer optional. With so much traffic coming from mobile devices, if your site isn't mobile-friendly, you're going to lose conversions. Make sure your content and forms are easy to interact with on smaller screens and that your pages load quickly.

CRO is all about taking what you've already built and making it better.

It's about understanding your customers and knowing your site so you can mold it to meet their needs. Every little tweak or change can lead to more conversions, better ROI, and an improved overall digital strategy. CRO isn't a game of "let's just try this"; it's a science of data, psychology, and experimentation that turns your digital experience into one where visitors become customers.

Content That Converts

Let's be honest—when it comes to Conversion Rate Optimization (CRO), content really is king. You can have the fastest website, the smoothest user interface, and all the AI in the world, but if your content falls flat, so will your conversions. In fact, in the race to win over customers, content isn't just the king—it's the whole royal family.

Storytelling: The Secret Sauce

First things first, people love stories. It's not just about selling a product; it's about selling the experience behind that product. Think about it: Would you rather read a product description that says "this chair is comfortable," or one that tells the story of how this chair is where you'll relax after a long day, read bedtime stories to your kids, and host Sunday brunches? When you weave storytelling into your content, you're tapping into emotion, and that's what drives people to take action.

For CRO, storytelling doesn't have to be a full-blown novel. It can be as simple as crafting relatable scenarios or highlighting customer success stories. When visitors can see themselves in your content, they're more likely to convert. Remember, facts tell, but stories sell.

Copy and Imagery: More Than Just Words and Pictures

Now let's talk about the right copy and imagery. Good copy isn't just about sounding smart—it's about being clear, compelling, and concise. You want to speak directly to your audience, not over their heads. If you can convey your value proposition in one strong sentence instead of three, you're already ahead of the game.

But copy alone won't cut it. You need visuals that complement your message. High-quality, relevant imagery can make or break a conversion. Think of it as setting the mood. If you're selling a premium product, your images better scream premium—no stock photos of fake-smiling people in a generic office setting. Your visuals should tell the same story your words are telling, creating a cohesive experience that makes your audience feel confident in clicking that "Buy Now" button.

Content Marketing: Playing the Long Game

Lastly, content marketing is the glue that holds everything together. You can have the best story, the sharpest copy, and the most stunning images, but if nobody sees them, what's the point? That's where content marketing comes in.

A strategic content marketing plan—whether it's through blog posts, social media, or e-mail campaigns—helps guide potential customers through the funnel. It's about building trust over time so that when they're ready to make a purchase, they think of you first. It's not a quick fix, but it's a powerful long-term strategy for CRO.

The Bottom Line

In the world of CRO, content is your best friend. It's what builds connections, creates trust, and ultimately gets people to take action. Whether through storytelling, the right copy and imagery, or a strong content marketing strategy, putting thought into your content is the key to turning visitors into loyal customers. So, yes—content really is king. And if you play it right, it'll lead your CRO strategy straight to the crown.

A/B Testing

A/B testing, at its core, is all about comparison. Think of it as a head-to-head competition between two versions of a web page, e-mail, or ad to determine which one performs better. It's a simple yet incredibly powerful concept for optimizing digital experiences and, more importantly, boosting conversion rates. Your priority is growth—whether that's increasing sales, leads, or engagement—and A/B testing is one of the most effective tools available to understand what truly drives your digital consumers to take action (Figure 9.1).

When discussing conversion rate optimization (CRO), you're essentially asking: How can you turn more of your website visitors into paying customers? A/B testing helps answer that by running controlled experiments. You can test two versions of a web page (Version A and Version B), with only one variable changed between them. For instance, Version A might have a red CTA button, while Version B uses a blue one. By presenting these versions to different segments of your audience and tracking their behavior, you can see which version results in more clicks, sign-ups, or purchases.

Here's where it gets exciting for you. A/B testing isn't just about adjusting button colors—it's about gaining a deeper understanding of your

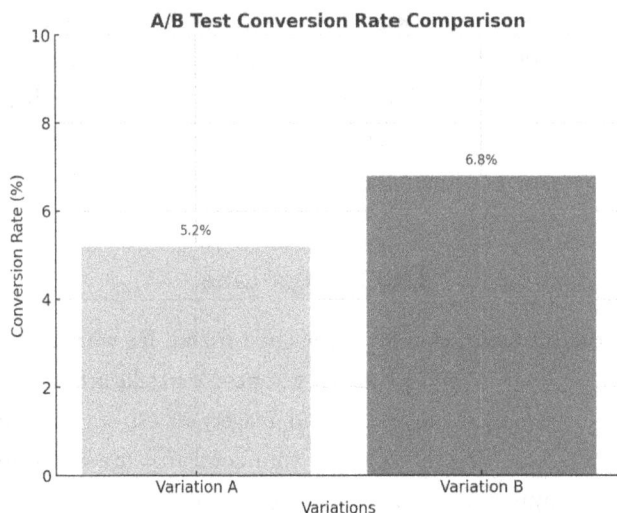

Figure 9.1 A/B testing example

consumers' behaviors and preferences. You get actionable insights into what works and what doesn't. It may not be the button color but the placement of an offer, the wording of a headline, or the images used in a campaign. Each test teaches you something valuable about what resonates with your customers, allowing you to make informed decisions based on real user behavior rather than assumptions.

You don't need to be involved in running these tests yourself, but understanding their value is key. A/B testing allows you to lead with confidence, knowing that your decisions are based on data, not guesses. It also helps you stay agile in a fast-paced digital environment. What worked last year—or even last month—may no longer be as effective today. With A/B testing, you can continuously iterate and improve, ensuring you're always optimizing the customer journey.

Moreover, A/B testing plays a crucial role in building trust with your customers. When you fine-tune your digital experiences, you're removing friction from their journey. The easier and more intuitive the experience, the more likely consumers are to convert. Every small improvement adds up over time to create a more seamless and satisfying interaction.

In the aspect of CRO, A/B testing helps you shift from broad generalizations to specific, tailored strategies that address your consumers' unique needs. It's your responsibility to champion data-driven decision-making within your organization. A/B testing offers the insights you need to better understand your digital consumers, leading to smarter investments, stronger customer relationships, and, ultimately, higher conversion rates. It's about knowing what works—and why—so you can lead your teams toward success in the digital marketplace.

Creating the A/B Recipe

Managing the minutiae and tabulating results of effective A/B testing is a daunting process if you don't have a clear plan in place. Follow these steps and you'll ensure you're doing the most you can for your digital marketing needs (Figure 9.2):

1. **Define Clear Objectives**
   Start by defining what you're looking to achieve. Are you attempting to increase click-through rates? Boost conversions? Improve user

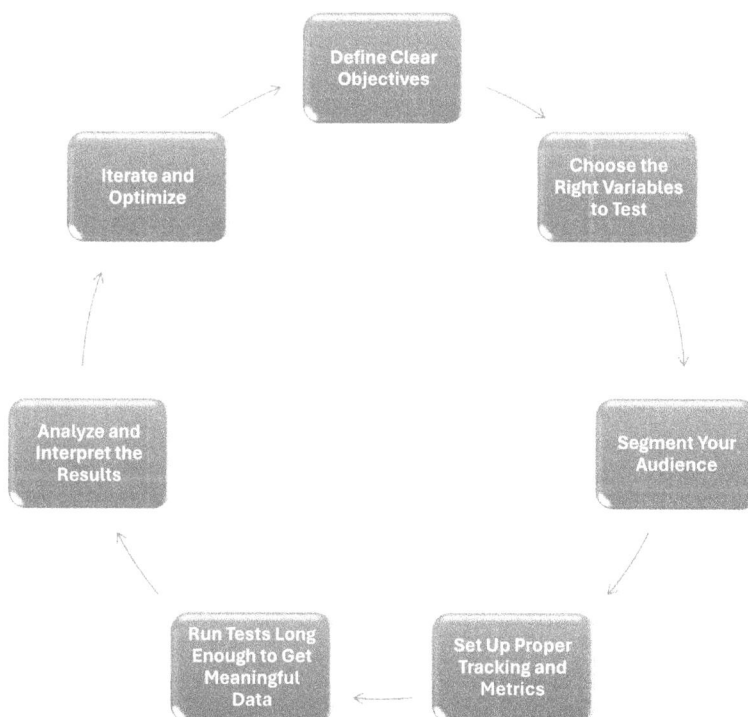

Figure 9.2 A/B testing strategy framework

experience? Determining what you want out of an A/B test ahead of time will help you stay on track and means your efforts will focus on what's most important for your business. It's like laying the groundwork—knowing what it looks like when you're successful before you begin.

2. **Choose the Right Variables to Test**

   Focus on things that directly affect user behavior: your headlines, buttons, the layout of your page, or the images included. Don't test more than one thing at a time—keep the number of variables you're testing to a minimum (you want to test just one thing at a time, like a red button vs. a blue button).

3. **Segment Your Audience**

   Not all customers are equally responsive, so the same version might appeal more to one segment than to another. If by showing Version A to one segment and Version B to another, you find that people in one (but not the other) respond better, you can target segments accordingly.

4. **Set Up Proper Tracking and Metrics**

   Set up your tracking tools accurately. If you are using Google Analytics and form goals and so on we'd be keen to see this pre-coffee, because then we'd know exactly what to measure (clicks, sign-ups, and sales) and, consequently, which version is performing better, in line with your goals.

5. **Run Tests Long Enough to Get Meaningful Data**

   Don't get test-weary. Let your experiments run long enough to deliver substantial data. Whenever you stop an experiment too early, you run the risk of manifesting your expectations about the result, especially if you display those expectations publicly. Aim for results that are statistically significant enough to inform your next step.

6. **Analyze and Interpret the Results**

   When you're done, take a look at your results. Which version of your ad, business, presentation, or product worked best and why? What do your consumers' behaviors tell you? With this knowledge, you can make changes and apply these lessons to other similar endeavors.

7. **Iterate and Optimize**

   However, A/B testing is not something that you do once and then forget about. Learn from each data point in your campaign to continually improve. Each aspect of each A/B test should be continuously honed to become more effective over time, and what you learn from one test could lead you to new ideas for other tests along the way as well. This is why being flexible and having a willingness to change is so important.

More importantly, if you take this approach, your A/B testing will not just improve your digital marketing efforts but will also be a true enabler of smarter, more data-driven decisions to achieve marketing goals in the long term.

A/B Testing Use Case: Improving Airline Booking Conversions

Let's say an airline wants to increase its online bookings. Here's a streamlined approach using A/B testing to achieve that goal.

1. **Define the Goal**
   The airline's goal is simple: increase the number of completed bookings. They also want to reduce cart abandonment, making the booking process smoother for users.
2. **Choose What to Test**
   The airline focuses on testing two key elements:
   - **CTA button:**
     1. **Version A**: "Book Now" in the airline's brand color.
     2. **Version B**: "Secure Your Seat" in a bold, contrasting color.
   - **Booking form:** Testing a **simplified form** versus a detailed one to see which leads to more completed bookings.
3. **Segment the Audience**
   The airline tests these changes on two groups:
   - **Frequent travelers** (loyalty members).
   - **First-time visitors** to the website.
     This helps them understand if different types of customers respond better to certain changes.
4. **Track the Right Metrics**
   They measure:
   - **Click-through rate (CTR)** from the homepage to the booking page.

- ○ **Conversion rate** for completed bookings.
- ○ **Cart abandonment rate**, tracking how many people start but don't finish booking.

5. **Run the Test for Meaningful Results**

They run the test over 2 weeks to gather enough data, accounting for different booking behaviors during peak times and off-peak times.

6. **Analyze Results**

- ○ The **"Secure Your Seat"** CTA results in a 12 percent increase in bookings from new visitors.
- ○ The **simplified booking form** reduces cart abandonment by 15 percent, especially on mobile devices.

7. **Optimize Based on Insights**

The airline rolls out the winning CTA across the site and implements the simplified booking form for mobile users, ensuring a smoother booking experience. By using A/B testing, the airline boosts its booking conversions and creates a more user-friendly experience, all driven by data and real user behavior.

Build the CRO Innovation Lab

Building a team of enthusiasts for A/B testing and conversion rate optimization (CRO) is like assembling a squad of data-driven superheroes. It's all about finding the right mix of curiosity, experimentation, and a relentless drive to improve. But here's the trick: Once you've got the team, turning them into an innovation lab is where the real fun begins. Let's break it down:

Step 1: Find the Right Enthusiasts

First things first, you need the right people. A/B testing and CRO aren't for the faint of heart—it's for those who love data and can geek out over small percentage increases. Look for team members who are:

- **Curious by Nature**: People who ask "what if" all the time. They're the ones who wonder, "What happens if we change this button color?" or "How can we improve that user flow?"

- **Data-Driven**: It's crucial your team loves diving into analytics and metrics. They should be comfortable running reports, understanding the results, and drawing actionable conclusions.
- **Creative Problem-Solvers**: Yes, it's about numbers, but creativity plays a huge role in testing and optimization. Find people who think outside the box when it comes to improving user experiences.
- **Collaborative**: A/B testing and CRO don't happen in silos. You need folks who can collaborate with designers, developers, and marketers without getting territorial.

Step 2: Set Clear Goals and Keep Things Fun

Once you have your dream team, it's time to set clear goals. Be explicit about what success looks like. Are you focused on increasing the conversion rate by 10 percent? Testing out new user experience strategies? Make sure everyone knows what they're working toward.

And don't forget to keep it fun. A/B testing is essentially a giant playground for digital marketers and product developers. Make it a game by rewarding creative test ideas or holding a "test of the week" contest. After all, everyone loves a little friendly competition.

Step 3: Foster a Culture of Experimentation

Here's where you begin turning your A/B testing team into an innovation lab. The goal isn't just to optimize—it's to foster a mindset of continual improvement. To do that:

- **Encourage Wild Ideas**: Don't just stick to safe, incremental changes. Push the team to test big, bold hypotheses. Even if the tests fail, you'll learn something new. Remember, there's no such thing as a "bad" test—just ones that teach you what *not* to do.
- **Test Everything**: Button color, headlines, pricing, checkout flow—you name it, you test it. If it's part of the customer experience, it's fair game for experimentation.

- **Celebrate Both Wins and Losses**: A/B testing is all about learning, not just winning. Celebrate the tests that tank as much as the ones that skyrocket conversions. Each failure is a step closer to cracking the code on your audience.

Step 4: Scale and Systematize

As your team starts racking up wins (and learning from those fails), it's time to systematize. Use tools like Trello or Asana to track tests, document results, and iterate on what works. This is how you go from a team that tests occasionally to a well-oiled optimization machine.

Step 5: Make It a Lab of Innovation

Now, to truly turn your team into an innovation lab, give them the freedom to experiment without fear. Empower them to challenge the status quo and question existing strategies. Create an environment where they can try crazy ideas without the fear of failure holding them back. Let them geek out on optimization theories, create prototypes, and go down data rabbit holes.

So, that's how you build an A/B testing and CRO dream team that evolves into an innovation lab: hire the right enthusiasts, create a testing culture, celebrate every experiment, and give them room to innovate. Just think of it as a continuous journey of small wins, occasional epic fails, and constant improvement—all in the name of conversion glory.

AI in All This

Let's talk about how AI is shaking up Conversion Rate Optimization (CRO) and A/B testing—like when your phone starts predicting what you're going to text before you even finish typing. If you've been around the CRO block, you know the classic A/B test: compare a red button to a blue button, swap a headline, and see which version makes people click more. But with AI in the picture, this process has leveled up, becoming faster, smarter, and way more effective.

AI: The Ultimate CRO Wingman

CRO is all about nudging users to take action, whether that's clicking "buy now," signing up for a newsletter, or checking out your TikTok. Traditionally, you'd run experiments, adjusting small parts of your website to see what works best. Now, AI has entered the chat, supercharging the process by predicting what changes will drive conversions before you've even run the test. Forget waiting for results—AI gives you the inside scoop upfront.

How AI Is Supercharging A/B Testing

AI isn't just making A/B testing quicker—it's turning it into a powerhouse. By analyzing huge datasets in seconds, it gives you actionable insights faster than your morning coffee kicks in.

- **Predictive Analysis**: Think of AI as your CRO fortune teller. It knows what's going to work and tells you which tests to prioritize. No more endless rounds of tweaking and waiting for results—AI cuts to the chase, telling you what changes will likely make the biggest difference.
- **Dynamic Personalization**: In traditional A/B testing, you show one group a red button, the other group a blue one, and hope for the best. AI takes it further by personalizing the button color in real-time for each user. One person sees red, another sees blue, based on what AI predicts will convert them best. It's like customization magic, but without any extra work.
- **Multivariate Testing on Overdrive**: If A/B testing is juggling two variables, multivariate testing is like juggling six. AI makes this complex testing a breeze by analyzing multiple elements at once (like your headlines, images, and calls t -action) to find the perfect combo for maximum conversions. What would take a human days, AI nails it in hours.

How A/B Testing Feeds AI's Brain

AI isn't all-knowing right out of the gate—it learns from the data you give it. And A/B tests provide the fuel for its learning engine. Every test run adds more data, teaching the AI what works, what doesn't, and how to improve.

- **Data Collection and Pattern Recognition**: Each A/B test feeds AI with valuable insights about user behavior. Over time, AI starts recognizing patterns—like a particular button color working best for a specific demographic. Eventually, AI doesn't even need to run the test; it just knows what's likely to work.
- **Continuous Learning**: AI is like that classmate who's always studying. Every test adds to its knowledge, making future predictions more accurate. It refines its understanding with every round, so the more you test, the smarter it gets.
- **Automated Testing and Optimization**: Tired of setting up tests and waiting for results? AI's got your back. It can automatically run and adjust tests in real-time based on user data. Think of it as your 24/7 CRO assistant, running tests and optimizing your site while you're binge-watching Netflix.
- **Personalization and Segmentation**: After running enough tests, AI can even personalize the user experience based on who's visiting your site. Minimalist design lovers get the clean look they crave, while feature-rich fanatics get the full experience. And all this happens without you lifting a finger.

The Bottom Line: AI + A/B Testing = CRO Perfection

AI isn't just streamlining A/B testing—it's turning it into a self-improving machine. Every test feeds the AI, making it smarter and faster, with predictions that help optimize your site before you even hit "run." Combining AI with A/B testing means you're not just improving conversions, you're building a growth engine that runs on autopilot. Now, if only AI could help us decide between tacos or pizza for dinner.

Key Points

- Reducing friction on your site, like slow load times or complex processes, helps users convert more easily.
- A/B testing provides data-driven insights to optimize website elements and improve conversion rates.
- AI enhances personalization by tailoring user experiences based on real-time behavior, increasing conversions.
- CRO is an ongoing process of testing and learning, with AI accelerating improvements and automation.

As We Move Ahead

Wow you did it! You got to this point in the book and, hopefully, your consumer through their journey into a conversion! Alright, the book is now done. Your did your job, sales closed, no need to worry about the consumer anymore….

Not really. There is still that little thing we like to call, *retention*. It's post-purchase time. The behavior of your digital consumer after their purchase is at times even more important than your strategy to get them to this point. The need to sustain a long-term relationship, assess their usage and satisfaction, and generate loyalty is critical. The next chapter will expose us to this in more detail.

CHAPTER 10

Building Digital Loyalty: Recipes for Retention

Well done is better than well said.

—*Benjamin Franklin*

Chapter Overview

Franklin's quote is a perfect reminder that actions speak louder than words, especially in post-purchase support. This chapter discusses how offering real, actionable help through efficient loyalty programs, upsell strategies, warranties, empathetic customer service, and clear product guidance builds trust and loyalty. It's not just about promising great service; it's about delivering it consistently, ensuring customers feel valued long after the sale.

The Real Relationship Begins

We call this "post-purchase behavior," the stage in the digital dating game that follows the transaction, when the consumer either becomes your biggest fan or … not. After the date, in the romance business equivalence, the consumer judges whether it worked out—whether the product was worth it; whether, for example, the delivery worked smoothly or felt like waiting for a space package to the moon. Satisfaction yields repeat business. Dissatisfaction results in whomp-you-down negative reviews. It's a game of odds, but you have to master the game.

This is where the magic—or mayhem—occurs. If the customer is happy with your purchase, they will likely make a repeat purchase, write a glowing review, or tell their friends. If not, that is where your customer service department suddenly finds itself flooded. This is the phase where your business should be making the most money. You closed the sale, everybody is happy, but the real question now becomes—how do you keep them coming back?

What then can you do to positively impact this important part of the buyer's journey? Communicate with customers about what's happening with their order. Send them the follow-up e-mail; toss in a promo code for their next purchase, and perhaps a request to review (the proper kinds, please). Take care of customers with these thoughtful touches to help ensure a happy camper. And remember, it's the twenty-first century, where complaining customers have more potential ways to make noise than ever before. On the other hand, happy customers might become your best free advertisers.

Put simply, post-purchase behavior is not a sideshow to purchase—it is where the real action occurs, the time when loyalty is gained or lost. Get it right and you'll spawn converts and advocates who come back for more.

Cognitive Dissonance

Cognitive Dissonance in the digital consumer age is that nagging feeling of regret that creeps in right after a purchase—the moment when customers start questioning whether they made the right choice. It's the digital version of buyer's remorse, amplified by the ease of comparison shopping and the endless stream of ads that follow us online. With so many options just a click away, it's easy for digital consumers to second-guess their decision. "added

Why does this happen? After a purchase, digital consumers are bombarded with information—ads for similar products, flash sales, or even better deals. Imagine buying a pair of running shoes only to immediately see an ad for a different pair with better reviews. Or purchasing a TV and finding out it's now on sale for hundreds less. According to a HubSpot survey, 81 percent of consumers trust online reviews as much as personal recommendations, so encountering new information can easily trigger post-purchase regret.

So, what can digital marketers do to minimize this dissonance?

- **Set the Right Expectations**: Ensure your product descriptions, images, and videos accurately reflect what customers will receive. Misleading content is a surefire way to create cognitive dissonance.

- **Follow-up Communication**: Send a post-purchase e-mail to reinforce the customer's decision. Highlight the benefits of their purchase and how it meets their needs.
- **Leverage Social Proof**: Display positive reviews and testimonials to reassure customers that others are happy with their decision, reducing their doubts.
- **Offer Easy Return Policies**: A hassle-free return process reduces post-purchase anxiety, giving customers peace of mind that they can change their mind if needed.
- **Amplify Customer Service**: Sometimes consumers just need a simple "it's ok" moment when they contact customer service with any grievances or negative feelings. A sale can be salvaged with trained experts on emotional intelligence, empathy, and sympathy.

By addressing cognitive dissonance proactively, digital marketers can create a more satisfying post-purchase experience and reduce buyer's remorse.

Theory to Practice

Digital strategists, however, need not be psychologists who pore over published research and spend days deciphering complicated equations—this is not our arena. However, if we understand a few theories that relate to cognitive dissonance, we have our very own secret "customer consumerism decoder ring" that can give us a tiny sneak peek behind the curtain of what goes on in a customer's brain when they do a little acrobatics over the purchase of your product. It's better if this does not include an actual backflip out of the shopping cart! The more we understand, the better we can help them to land on their feet.

Cognitive Dissonance Theory (Leon Festinger, 1957)

Consumers feel uneasy when their buying decision forces them to reconcile thoughts and actions that don't match up. Usually, dissonance gives rise to a desire to change one or the other (i.e., their thoughts or realities).

For instance, maybe someone felt bad for maxing out her credit card on a fancy new smartwatch. But rather than let those negative thoughts linger, she might persuade herself it was the right move ("Good for my health in the long run") and then go online to help herself along by hunting high and low for positive reviews.

Self-Perception Theory (Daryl Bem, 1972)

There's no need to feel uncomfortable with having conflicting thoughts: People look at their actions and work out what they think about it by observing what they have done. Feeling pleased with a splurge purchase, a consumer might think: "I must really like this brand" or "It's a great product, I just bought it" (if they feel bad about the expenditure—another alternative would be: "It hadn't crossed my mind to try it out before, but now I feel good as I have just bought it!") Instead of feeling uncertain about how they feel, they work out how they feel by looking at what they did.

Balance Theory (Fritz Heider, 1946)

The idea here is that people and things they like need to stay balanced with each other. If a consumer likes a social media influencer who likes a new skincare product, that person will also like the product more. But if they don't like the product after all—say, if they fail to see any real results—they will either downgrade how much they liked the influencer or rationalize how much better the product actually is to make their range of evaluations balance out.

So, these theories help to elucidate the role consumers play in modifying their behaviors and their thinking—especially when it comes to sheer multitude of possibilities present when making decisions in the digital marketplace.

Reviews and Testimonials: The Ugly, the Bad, the Good

The Ugly

Yes, I am offering this in the reverse order, because we need to get ugly out of the way first. The ultimate goal of managing buyer's remorse is simple:

Keep your customers happy and avoid them turning into keyboard warriors with bad reviews, complaints, or (worse) horror-story testimonials. No one wants to wake up to a one-star review that reads, "I should've just stuck with my old toaster," right?

By addressing cognitive dissonance, you can help customers feel like they made the right choice, dodging that uncomfortable post-purchase regret. Think of it like damage control before the damage happens: If they feel good about their buy, they won't be leaving reviews that sound like they bought a haunted vacuum!

So, the next time someone second-guesses that new gadget, you swoop in with a little reassurance (maybe a follow-up e-mail with tips or an extra perk) before they vent their regrets on Yelp. Save the day—and your brand's reputation—one happy customer at a time!

The Bad

Sure, reviews here and there are awesome—and a hard-earned gold star for your digital business! But if we aren't consistently growing those glowing reviews, well, the decline can be steep. It can hinder retention, slow the onboarding of new business, and give a bad first impression to prospective customers. After all, who wants to walk into a business with "meh, this isn't bad" vibes? If your review section is a ghost town or populated with equivocal reviews, you're setting up a "so-so" environment, which isn't particularly inspiring to the people who already love you and aren't exactly welcoming to new, potential buyers. You want your digital presence to be a place people want to talk up, not be indifferent to or, even worse, actively avoid due to unchecked bad experiences. Keep those reviews coming, and you aren't just growing a business—you're growing a community of happy, loyal customers!

The Good

Consumers heavily rely on online reviews when deciding whether or not to make a purchase. In fact, a whopping 91.1 percent of consumers read at least one review before committing to a product, with more than half (54.7 percent) reading four or more reviews before making their final decision. These reviews significantly influence purchasing behavior, with 77 percent of shoppers specifically seeking out websites that display customer reviews (PowerReviews 2023; Capital One Shopping 2024)

Consistent, positive, and quality reviews aren't a nice-to-have anymore—they've become critical to growing a digital business. It's no coincidence that good reviews help to establish trust, enhance your credibility, and are often the deciding factor for a potential customer who is checking you out for the first time. And most people are much more likely to trust a business with a number of great reviews than one with just a handful. Reviews are social proof, and, in today's digital marketplace where every potential buyer is looking for validation before committing to a purchase, they are critical.

Steps for Success

- **Alert**: For us digital strategists, hoping for reviews is not enough. We need to inspire and even force consumers to write them. How? Here we can be creative:
- **Easy and Painless:** The more you make it easy for customers to leave a review, the better. After a purchase or service has been completed, send an e-mail to the customer asking them to take some time out and leave a review by providing a link to the review page. Make it short and sweet.
- **Rewarding Feedback:** What's free and motivating? A discount code, complimentary shipping, or an entry into a prize draw for leaving a review. But make sure it's genuine—people smell a rat from a mile away.
- **Timing Is Everything:** Ask people when they're feeling the happiest they'll ever feel after using your product or receiving your service. Then give them a little nudge.
- **Make the Ask Personal:** Instead of a generic "Please leave us a review," add a little personalization, such as "We'd like to hear how you're finding using [the specific product or service]."
- **Use Social Media:** Entice people to review you on social networks such as Facebook or Google where they are most likely to engage. Say thanks and give a shout-out to people who have previously reviewed you, to inspire them to do so again.

With these tactics, you don't merely solicit reviews; you incite and prod consumers toward the kinds of feedback that swell our digital footprint and bolster the standing of the brand.

Loyalty Programs

Face it—digital is noisy. Loyalty programs are what can really shine to make your brand stand out in the crowd, to be your free side dish with an Extra Value Meal. Loyalty programs are an integral part of stimulating purchases among digital consumers in the post-purchase consumer behaviors. This is the reason why it's important:

- **Encourages Repeat Purchase:** Loyalty programs encourage the quest for more, keeping people motivated to return to your brand by offering rewards and perks that build ongoing value well beyond the initial purchase. This creates a state of habitual buy behavior and lessens the possibility of customers switching over to your competitor.
- **Increases Customer Lifetime Value:** The relevance of personalized rewards and exclusive offers keeps customers connected to your brand, increasing the monetary and emotional value that the customer brings to the brand over time, with more frequent, higher-value buys.
- **Greater Brand Loyalty:** Happy and engaged customers who are part of a strong rewards program will organically promote your brand, creating a series of referrals and word-of-mouth usage.
- **Increases Value:** When customers feel valued by a brand, it forms an emotional bond that means that they are less likely to be price-sensitive and more likely to engage in long-term relationships. They are also more likely to stick with a brand and not even consider the competition.

Simply put, an effective loyalty program can make a one-time buyer a customer for life, improving the experience for both the consumer and the brand alike.

The most compelling loyalty programs do precisely what digital consumers demand: They wrap exclusive rewards, special offers, and slick online experiences in one easy-to-access, endlessly configurable package, usually with a dashboard style app in which a digital consumer can track points or perks and be acutely aware that they are a part of select tribe. A Loyalty Report from 2022 stated that 86 percent of consumers rate simplicity and ease of use as the most important attributes in a loyalty program. This indicates that consumers value straightforward, user-friendly experiences when engaging in loyalty initiatives. You will be amazed at how much longer customers will stick around and how much more they will spend and how many more of their friends will join them when they feel this way. It's a virtuous cycle.

Now, the next step, if you're really playing the loyalty game right, is using your customer data to keep things fresh and relevant. Don't let your rewards program get stale—keep reengineering it to reflect "what's hot" and up to the minute. Think of it as a fashion statement: last season's rewards are out, and the ones your customers actually care about, in.

And digital outlets? Well, digital channels are your buds here. E-mail, mobile apps, and social media are the popular kids that remind consumers they've got rewards waiting or deals that they can't afford to miss. It's like breadcrumbs—but only way better.

But here's the trick: Make it fun! Gamify it! What's not to love about leveling up? Every shopping trip should feel like completing the next level of a videogame (if you don't make the user interface too complicated). Don't make it hard. People want easy. Give them a friction-free experience and they'll keep coming back for more.

But how do you measure magic? The metrics to watch out for are retention rates, purchase frequency, and engagement. If your program delivers the goods in these three ways, consider yourself a happy camper. Which is not to say good brands rest on their laurels. They are forever improving their loyalty programs to stay on people's radars and remain sticky.

Ultimately, then, loyalty programs are about relationships, and relationships do take work—but what choice do you have? Get the moves right (and the digital channels will help), and you will create the kind of bond among consumers that lasts for years to come. Less like an affair than a marriage or any long-term love relationship, the benefits really are mutual.

Upselling and Cross-Selling

Upselling and cross-selling are excellent sales opportunities during the post-purchase phase. There is no better time to suggest related or complementary products, as these recommendations feel natural and helpful to the customer. For example, suggesting a laptop bag after a laptop purchase is more effective than offering unrelated items. This strategy not only boosts the average order value but also reinforces the customer's purchase decision.

Here are the top 10 digital marketing tactics for promoting upselling and cross-selling, with examples for each:

- **Personalized E-mail Campaigns**: Send a follow-up e-mail with product recommendations based on the customer's purchase history.
  1. Example: A customer buys a smartphone, and the follow-up e-mail suggests a phone case or screen protector.
- **In-App Notifications**: Use app notifications to suggest relevant items post-purchase.
  1. Example: A food delivery app suggests dessert or drinks after the main meal is ordered.
- **Thank-You Pages**: Display complementary products on the order confirmation page.
  1. Example: After purchasing a gaming console, the thank-you page suggests a controller or game.
- **Chatbots and AI**: Use chatbots to make real-time product recommendations during or after the purchase.
  1. Example: A chatbot recommends workout gear after a customer buys running shoes.
- **Dynamic Popups**: Show popups with relevant product suggestions during checkout.
  1. Example: A fashion site suggests accessories that complement the dress in the shopping cart.
- **Product Bundling**: Offer discounts on bundled products sold together.
  1. Example: An electronics store bundles a camera, tripod, and memory card for a discount.

- **Customer Loyalty Programs**: Reward repeat purchases with special offers on complementary products.
  1. Example: A cosmetics brand offers loyalty points that can be redeemed for related products like skincare.
- **Exit-Intent Popups**: Display relevant product suggestions before a customer leaves the site.
  1. Example: A home décor site offers a discount on throw pillows to match the sofa the customer viewed.
- **Retargeting Ads**: Show related products to customers who recently made a purchase.
  1. Example: After buying a bicycle, a customer sees ads for helmets or bike locks on social media.
- **Social Media Engagement**: Use interactive content to encourage customers to explore complementary products.
  1. Example: An apparel brand uses Instagram Stories to showcase how to style new purchases with complementary items.

These tactics make upselling and cross-selling feel natural and helpful, ultimately enhancing both customer satisfaction and business revenue.

Post-Purchase Customer Support

Customer Service: Handling Concerns with Care

We all know that it takes so much blood, sweat, and tears to get a customer, so what happens after the purchase is just as important, even more important—because it is here that we either seal the deal with consumers for life or send them to the dark purgatory of "I'll never buy here again." First, and most obvious: customer service.

The thought of being bounced around a robot-like call center and going through endless buttons before someone gives you a script-like response and refuses to listen to what you want to say does not speak well of your brand. Whether it is a query about an ordered item, a troubleshooting tip, or, worse, a faulty product, clients want to know they can rely on the know-how and empathy of your support team; it can be the difference between a good and bad experience. Think about it: They not only need a solution; they also need to know that we care enough to get it right. And, yes, a bit of empathy does not hurt either—after all, who wants to speak to a robot when you're super upset?

Warranty and Installation Services: Peace of Mind

Warranty and installation services. Extended warranties are not just about insurance in case of a product defect. It is a feeling. People want to feel safe, and if something goes wrong, hey, we have got your back. Installation services? Stellar. It is for everyone who is not tech-savvy. A walk-through here, an "I'll do it for you" there … it is us saying: "We want this to work for you." That's trust and loyalty right there.

Returns: Hassle-Free, Stress-Free

And, of course, returns. They will come, but they don't have to be painful. A smooth returns process acts as insurance—if customers know that they'll never be stuck with a product they don't want or need, they'll feel safer spending their money with us. The easier it is, the more likely they are to return.

Technical Guidance and Education: Helping Customers Succeed

There's technical expertise and education: Whether through how-to videos, online FAQs, or one-on-one guidance, making it easier for a customer to use their product properly reinforces their purchase, which leads to a happy customer. We don't just want to sell products; we want people to be receptive and satisfied with a product long after they've purchased it.

Ultimately, good post-purchase support is the secret to turning a one-time buyer into a zealous evangelist. When your customers feel looked after and appreciated, they don't just stick around them, they tell others. And that's the kind of brand loyalty we all want.

AI in All This

One of the most significant aspects of using AI is that it dramatically enhances the post-purchase communication between businesses and customers. Through AI, there's hardly any friction in the communication channels that exist post-sale. The need to constantly communicate with customers after they've purchased something is widespread for every industry. Customers expect to be kept in the loop in terms of order updates, delivery information, and much more. Deploying AI for such purposes has become critical in today's context. For instance, using AI-driven chatbots can greatly enhance customer engagement and also form one of the primary communication streams between businesses and customers. It is ideal for answering customers' frequently asked questions promptly and for essential troubleshooting efforts.

In terms of customer support, AI helps in reducing the time it takes to resolve concerns. It's able to do this by routing customers to either a guide or a FAQ page or a live support agent. Essentially, it spots the type of concern quickly and then delivers it to the right resource. In the process, it speeds up the time it takes for a customer to get the help they need. Second, AI can identify patterns in a customer's behavior that indicate when they might need help. This is quite valuable for companies as it allows them to get ahead of customer concerns and offer support before things become a problem.

AI also makes it easier to handle warranties, returns, and product recommendations. With automated reminders, customers spend less time being nudged for a replacement; with customer-friendly returns, it gets easier to earn customer respect and return custom; and with options for upselling and cross-selling based on the data, AI turns one-time buyers into lifelong customers with personalized recommendations that keep them satisfied. AI helps businesses provide the support and options customers want, so they can be confident that they have a solution that serves their needs every time.

Key Points

- Post-purchase behavior is key to keeping customers happy and loyal, while unhappy customers can leave bad reviews.
- Clear communication after a purchase, like order updates and thank-you e-mails, helps keep customers satisfied.

- Easy returns, warranties, and installation services make customers feel safe about their purchase.
- Following up with support and showing positive reviews helps stop customers from regretting their decision.
- Good post-purchase care turns customers into fans who recommend your brand to others.

As We Move Ahead

Buckle up, because in the next chapter, we're diving into *Performance Measurement: The GPS to Success*. Think of it like your trusty navigation app, but for business strategy—guiding you through the twists and turns of metrics, key performance indicators (KPIs), and data-driven decisions to make sure you're always on the right path. We'll explore how to avoid the dreaded "recalculating" when things go off course and how to use performance insights to accelerate toward your goals. So, get ready to turn those numbers into a roadmap for victory, because success isn't just a destination; it's a well-measured journey.

CHAPTER 11

Performance Measurement: The GPS to Success

Not everything that counts can be counted, and not everything that can be counted counts.

—Albert Einstein

Chapter Overview

Just as Einstein warns against prioritizing the easily measurable over the truly valuable, this chapter underscores that effective digital strategy depends on carefully selecting metrics that reflect customer behavior, engagement, and growth, ensuring that digital efforts remain focused, purposeful, and impactful.

The Power of Data

The Internet, advanced software, and easy access to data have leveled the playing field for companies. But more data brings more responsibility in accessing, storing, and using it. You don't just need data—you need reliable, valuable information that helps you strategize, create a better customer experience, and stay ahead of the competition.

Why Digital Analytics Matters

Digital analytics brings data to life, giving you a clear understanding of what's happening inside your business and how it aligns with your objectives. Analyzing data across areas like sales, operations, forecasting, and marketing shows you where you're getting it right with customers—and where you're not. It's an essential tool for making informed, strategic decisions and is foundational to any successful business plan.

What Is Digital Analytics?

Digital analytics involves gathering, storing, and analyzing data collected from online platforms like websites, social media, and mobile apps. It provides insights into how users engage with your digital platforms by providing both qualitative data (how users feel about your brand) and quantitative data (real numbers and behaviors). For instance, qualitative data might capture user satisfaction, while quantitative data show visits or clicks.

In short, digital analytics empowers marketing, web development, and sales teams to make informed decisions based on actionable data.

The Evolution of Digital Analytics

Digital analytics took off with the Internet boom. Previously, businesses relied on simple transactional data, like sales figures or customer surveys, to make decisions. But the Internet introduced a wealth of real-time data that could reveal exactly what was happening behind the scenes. Companies quickly realized they needed more than sales data to understand online customer behavior—they needed insights into the entire user journey, from discovery to purchase.

As digital channels like social media and e-commerce grew, so did the demand for analytics that could track and interpret this data. The digitalization of analytics ushered in a new era where quick insights and adaptability became essential to business success.

Data Management in Digital Analytics

With the rise of Big Data, information has taken on new dimensions, often categorized by the "Three Vs":

1. **Volume:** The massive amount of data generated each day.
2. **Variety:** Different types of data, such as structured (like databases) and unstructured (like social media).
3. **Velocity:** The speed at which data are created and need to be processed.

To manage Big Data effectively, companies need specialized tools and methodologies. Here are some best practices:

1. **Only Use Data That Matter:** Focus on collecting data that are relevant to your strategy.
2. **Choose the Right Tools:** Platforms like Hadoop and Spark are designed to handle large volumes of data.
3. **Create Data Governance Policies:** Establish guidelines for consistent, ethical data usage.
4. **Visualize Data:** Use data visualization to make insights easier to understand.
5. **Invest in Training:** Educate employees on handling and interpreting data.
6. **Optimize Data Processing:** Keep data processing efficient.
7. **Secure Data:** Protect information with encryption and secure storage practices.

Tags and Structured Versus Unstructured Data

Tag management solutions help companies track visitor data and behavior by managing code embedded in websites. These tools streamline data collection without slowing down website performance.

Understanding **structured data** (organized, like a spreadsheet) versus **unstructured data** (more freeform, like customer reviews) is crucial for building an analytics system. Structured data are easier to process, while unstructured data can be challenging but provide valuable insights (Figure 11.1).

Data Quality

When it comes to data, quality is nonnegotiable. Good data are more than just a collection of numbers—they are data that are complete, accurate, and reliable, providing a true reflection of your business landscape. Data quality is essential for making sound business decisions because every insight, forecast, and strategy hinges on the integrity of the data

Structured Data	Unstructured Data
Highly organized in a predefined format	Lacks a predefined structure or format
Easily stored in relational databases	Challenging to store in traditional databases
Easily searchable using SQL queries	Requires advanced tools for searching and analysis
Examples: Spreadsheets, SQL databases	Examples: Emails, social media posts, videos
High data integrity and consistency	Varied data quality and may lack consistency

Figure 11.1 Structured vs. unstructured data

you use. Poor-quality data, on the other hand, can lead to misguided decisions, missed opportunities, and even financial losses.

To maintain data quality, you need to establish standards for data accuracy, completeness, consistency, and timeliness. **Accuracy** ensures that data reflect real-world facts, while **completeness** guarantees all necessary information is included. **Consistency** means that data align across all platforms and departments, reducing contradictions and confusion. **Timeliness** ensures data are current and relevant, which is especially crucial for real-time decisions in fast-paced industries.

Data integrity goes hand-in-hand with quality, encompassing the processes that keep your data secure, trustworthy, and free from unauthorized changes. This means setting up robust systems for data governance, security, and validation to protect against inaccuracies and fraud. In a world where data drive everything from customer insights to competitive strategy, ensuring data quality and integrity isn't just a good practice—it's a strategic advantage that helps your business make informed, impactful decisions.

Data Sources

To understand a consumer's digital journey, you need data from various sources. Here are some of the most common types:

1. **Online and In-Store Data:** Combining digital and physical sales data gives insights into customer habits and needs.

2. **Web Browsing Analytics:** Tracking what users do on your site connects online activity to sales.

3. **Surveys:** Data from surveys, like satisfaction scores and Net Promoter Scores (NPS), provide insights into customer sentiment.

4. **Customer Service Analytics:** Measuring service interactions can gauge support levels and identify areas for improvement.

5. **Marketing Platform Data:** Platforms like CRMs capture customer behavior, revealing what's working—and what's not—in your posts and campaigns.

6. **Loyalty Analytics:** Insights from loyalty programs show why customers keep coming back.

7. **Legacy Data:** Historical data help track how customer behaviors shift over time.

Additional Data Sources

Other sources, such as **web server logs** (raw website traffic) and **cookies** (tracking individual users), expand the scope of digital analytics. With the right tools, you can use these sources to detect trends, discover insights, and optimize your digital strategy.

Digital analytics isn't just about numbers; it's about understanding the experiences, preferences, and challenges of your customers. With a solid analytics platform, you can transform data into actionable insights, make smarter decisions, and build a competitive edge. Whether it's structured data or customer insights, digital analytics equips your teams with the knowledge they need to drive better decisions, keep customers happy, and, ultimately, fuel business growth.

Metrics

Metrics are the numbers that help you keep score, showing how well your business is doing in various areas—from how long people stick around on your website to how many actually click that "Buy Now" button. Think of metrics as the heartbeat of your strategies, giving you real-time updates on what's working and what might need a little tweaking. For example, in digital marketing, metrics like page views, click-through rates, and time on site tell you if your message is landing or getting lost in the noise.

But here's the thing—not all metrics are created equal. Enter Key Performance Indicators, or KPIs. While every KPI is a metric, not every metric gets the honor of being a KPI. KPIs are the VIPs of metrics, the ones that tie directly to your big-picture goals. They're called "key" for a reason! For instance, while page views are handy to track, it only becomes a KPI if boosting page views is essential to hitting a primary target, like increasing brand visibility or driving up sales.

So, why does this distinction matter? Because metrics give you the full picture, while KPIs zoom in on the stuff that moves the needle. By zeroing in on KPIs, you can avoid drowning in data and instead focus on the numbers that directly impact your goals. Knowing the difference between metrics and KPIs helps you stay laser-focused, track the right data, and make smarter, results-driven decisions without getting bogged down by every little stat.

Before we discuss how to identify the right metrics, it's important to know the foundation of the 20 most common digital behavior metrics used to evaluate consumer behavior experiences and strategies (Figure 11.2):

To leverage digital analytics for your business, consider metrics as the guide to strategic success. Good metrics serve as your navigator, ensuring every decision is data-driven, aligned with business goals, and steering you in the right direction.

Success Measures: Your Digital Metrics

Analytics are the cornerstone of any successful digital plan. Without them, it's like driving cross-country with no map—you might get somewhere, but who knows if it's where you wanted to go. With the right metrics, you'll know how your customers are responding, how well your campaigns are performing, and whether you need to adjust your strategy. When data are transformed into actionable information, your team doesn't just respond; they act decisively.

Strategic Metrics: More Than Just Numbers

Metrics aren't simply numbers—they tell a story about how customers interact with your brand. Think of them as storytelling tools that allow you to see and predict customer interactions with your digital assets. Good metrics create connections across campaigns, anticipate challenges, and allow you to make timely adjustments. They also provide stakeholders a common ground for data-led decisions, whether they're data experts or casual observers. Your job? Choose metrics that are both insightful and easily understood so everyone immediately knows what actions to take.

Metric	Definition	Example Calculation
Website Traffic	The total number of visitors to a website over a specific period.	Total Visitors: 10,000
Bounce Rate	The percentage of visitors who leave the website after viewing only one page.	Single Page Visitors: 4,000 / Total Visitors: 10,000 = 40%
Time on Site	The average duration a visitor spends on the website.	Total Time: 500,000 seconds / Total Sessions: 2,000 = 250 seconds (4 min 10 sec)
Pages per Session	The average number of pages a user views during a session.	Total Page Views: 8,000 / Total Sessions: 2,000 = 4 pages/session
Conversion Rate	The percentage of visitors who complete a desired goal (e.g., making a purchase).	Conversions: 300 / Visitors: 5,000 = 6%
Cart Abandonment Rate	The percentage of shopping carts abandoned before completing the purchase.	Abandoned Carts: 700 / Initiated Checkouts: 1,000 = 70%
Customer Lifetime Value (CLV)	The predicted net profit attributed to the entire future relationship with a customer.	Average Order Value: $100 x Purchase Frequency: 5 x Avg. Customer Lifespan: 2 years = $1,000
Email Open Rate	The percentage of recipients who open an email out of the total number sent.	Emails Opened: 1,200 / Emails Sent: 3,000 = 40%
Social Media Engagement	The level of interaction (likes, shares, comments) on social media posts.	Total Engagements: 500 / Total Posts: 10 = 50 engagements/post
Click-through Rate (CTR)	The percentage of users who click on a link out of the total who viewed it.	Clicks: 250 / Impressions: 10,000 = 2.5%

Figure 11.2 Main digital consumer metrics

What Makes a Good Metric?

Not every number is valuable. An effective metric should be more than descriptive; it must add meaning, context, and direction. Here's what you need:

- **Comparative:** Metrics should reveal patterns. Comparing user demographics or customer segments shows what's working and what isn't.

- **Clear to Read:** Metrics must be understandable to everyone, from the CEO to the analytics team. If you need a translator, the data won't drive action.
- **Ratio or Rate:** Ratios (e.g., views per user, engagement rate) offer a "health check" that's more insightful than isolated numbers, showing trends up, down, or steady.
- **Behavioral Motivation:** Metrics should indicate whether your strategy motivates desired actions, like newsletter sign-ups, product purchases, or website revisits.
- **Benchmarkable:** Compare metrics against industry benchmarks to assess if your strategy is effective or needs adjustment.
- **Easy to Manage:** Choose metrics that adapt as your strategy evolves. If a metric doesn't change with your actions, it may not be the right one.
- **Contextual:** Connect metrics to your strategic goals, ensuring they're action-driven rather than just report-driven.

Metrics that meet these criteria are more than numbers—they provide a roadmap for action, allow for on-the-go adjustments, and keep your digital campaign on track.

Balancing Behavioral and Financial Metrics

Digital success depends on more than isolated data points; it relies on metrics that connect the dots between consumer behavior and financial impact. Blending behavioral and financial metrics is the key to understanding not only *what* users do but also *why* they do it and how these actions influence profitability. This approach provides a comprehensive view of performance that helps businesses fine-tune strategies to drive engagement, boost customer satisfaction, and increase revenue.

How to Balance Behavioral and Financial Metrics

- **Define Key Behavioral Metrics:** Start by identifying behavioral metrics that reveal how users interact with your brand. Metrics like time on site, pages per session, bounce rate, and click-through rate (CTR) can indicate which aspects of your digital presence are attracting attention and where users might be losing interest. These metrics provide a window into user preferences, helping you understand which content, products, or features resonate most.

- **Set Financial Performance Indicators:** Next, establish financial metrics that measure your return on digital investments. Revenue, conversion rate, customer lifetime value (CLV), and return on ad spend (ROAS) are common indicators of financial health in digital strategy. These metrics ensure that each action aligns with revenue goals, giving you insight into the financial impact of your strategies.

- **Link Behavioral Metrics to Financial Outcomes:** The real value of balancing these metrics lies in their integration. Look for patterns between behavioral and financial data to see how one drives the other. For instance, if you notice that users who spend more time on the site are more likely to make a purchase, focus on increasing engagement to boost sales.

- **Use Predictive Analytics to Optimize Strategy:** Predictive analytics can reveal trends that help optimize campaigns. By analyzing past behavior, you can forecast future actions, such as which types of users are most likely to convert. These insights enable you to tailor your digital strategy to maximize the behaviors that drive financial outcomes.

- **Continuously Test and Refine:** A balanced metric strategy isn't static. Use A/B testing to compare different approaches and refine strategies based on real-time results. If increasing product recommendations per session improves both time on site (behavioral) and average order value (financial), for example, you'll know this tactic adds measurable value.

Case Study: Netflix's Use of Behavioral and Financial Metrics

Netflix is an excellent example of a company that balances behavioral and financial metrics to optimize digital consumer behavior. The streaming giant doesn't just rely on subscription counts (a financial metric) to evaluate success; it dives into behavioral data to understand what drives engagement and, ultimately, revenue.

- **Behavioral Metrics:** Netflix tracks detailed behavioral metrics such as viewing time, content selection, completion rates, and user interactions (e.g., liking or disliking content). By analyzing viewing patterns, Netflix identifies which genres, actors, or shows capture attention and keep users engaged. For instance, if a significant number of users watch thriller movies in the evening, Netflix's algorithms may prioritize promoting similar content during these hours to enhance user engagement.

- **Financial Metrics:** Netflix also measures financial success through subscriber growth, churn rate (the rate at which subscribers cancel), and revenue per user. By correlating engagement data with these financial metrics, Netflix understands which content investments lead to the highest return. For example, if a new show significantly increases viewer engagement but has minimal impact on new subscriptions or reduces churn, Netflix can better assess its contribution to the bottom line.

- **Integrating Behavioral and Financial Data:** Netflix doesn't view behavioral and financial data in isolation. Instead, the company examines how behavioral metrics like viewing frequency and session length influence subscriber retention and growth. If data show that highly engaged viewers are less likely to cancel subscriptions, Netflix prioritizes content that increases engagement among at-risk users. This balance ensures that content not only entertains but also drives long-term profitability by reducing churn.

- **Predictive Analytics and Testing:** Netflix uses predictive analytics to recommend content based on user behavior, forecasting which shows are likely to keep viewers engaged. By recommending content aligned with user preferences, Netflix increases time on the platform, which often correlates with lower churn and higher lifetime value. The company also tests everything—from user interface changes to content recommendations—to ensure that each feature positively impacts both engagement and revenue.

Benefits of a Balanced Metric Strategy

By integrating behavioral and financial metrics, businesses create a holistic view of the customer journey, leading to insights that support more strategic decisions. Companies can tailor their content, improve user experiences, and allocate resources more effectively, all while driving revenue growth. Netflix's approach demonstrates how a balance between these metrics helps create a cycle of continuous improvement: engagement enhances retention, and retention boosts profitability.

A balanced approach to digital analytics gives companies a powerful toolkit for understanding both the "what" and "why" of user actions. By examining how behavioral metrics drive financial outcomes, businesses can create data-informed strategies that not only meet customer needs but also maximize value.

Attribution Modeling

Attribution modeling is like a roadmap for your marketing campaigns, showing how every touchpoint—whether it's a paid ad, an e-mail, or a social post—contributes to your digital consumer's journey. Instead of looking at each channel in isolation, attribution modeling helps you see the whole ecosystem, making it easier to understand what's driving results and what's just along for the ride. This approach provides a clearer view of how each channel adds value, helping you make more strategic decisions about budget and resource allocation.

Attribution Modeling 101: How It Works

At its core, attribution modeling gives you insight into how each part of your campaign performs and interacts. It's often divided into two main approaches: **rule-based** and **data-driven** attribution.

- **Rule-Based Attribution:** This is the traditional approach, applying set rules to distribute credit across channels. It's simpler and gives you a big-picture look at how different channels contribute, but it often requires some trial and error to get right. Here are a few common models within this approach:

- **Linear Model:** This model gives equal credit to each touchpoint along the customer journey. If you're trying to keep your brand top of mind—especially in a competitive space—the linear model shows how each channel plays a role in maintaining customer engagement.
- **First Interaction Model:** In this model, the first touchpoint receives all the credit, which is perfect for identifying which channels are the most effective at building initial awareness.
- **Position-Based Model:** This approach splits credit between early and late touchpoints. For example, it gives more weight to the first interaction (awareness) and the last interaction (conversion), making it ideal if you're focused on both attracting new customers and driving sales.
- **Custom Attribution Model:** When you want a model that reflects your unique marketing strategy, custom attribution lets you create a framework that incorporates elements from various rule-based models. It's highly customizable, which means it's excellent for brands with complex, multichannel strategies.
- **Data-Driven Attribution:** Unlike rule-based attribution, data-driven attribution relies on algorithms to evaluate each touchpoint's unique value. Service providers use proprietary algorithms to analyze vast amounts of data across multiple customer journeys, calculating the precise impact of each interaction on your bottom line. This method is particularly powerful because it removes guesswork and offers a data-backed look at where your campaigns have the most impact.

Why You Need Attribution Modeling

Attribution modeling lets you see how every dollar you spend contributes to the customer journey and, ultimately, to your revenue. By taking a data-driven approach, you avoid the pitfalls of focusing on just one channel or metric. Here's how it benefits you:

8. **Optimize Budgets with Confidence:** By understanding which channels contribute most to conversions, you can make informed budget adjustments. If paid search is driving most of your

conversions, you might allocate more funds there and scale back on underperforming channels.

9. **Prevent Channel Conflict:** Attribution modeling eliminates the issue of channels competing for recognition, ensuring you get a holistic view of your marketing impact. Instead of putting too much focus on the price or individual values of each channel, you can see how they work together as part of a larger strategy.

10. **Enhance Future Campaigns:** With data-driven attribution, you don't just see what worked—you also get predictive insights into what's likely to work in future campaigns. By applying these insights, you can build campaigns that are more effective from the start, maximizing engagement and conversions.

Real-Life Example: How Netflix Uses Attribution Modeling

Take Netflix, for example. Netflix doesn't just track subscriber numbers; it monitors everything from content preferences and viewing patterns to how subscribers interact with recommendations. The company uses a combination of rule-based and data-driven attribution to understand not only which channels bring in new subscribers but also what keeps them engaged and reduces churn.

Netflix's linear and custom attribution models track engagement metrics across touchpoints, from social ads to e-mail notifications, which help the company adjust its recommendation algorithms and inform content investments. Data-driven models take this a step further by analyzing how each interaction impacts retention rates, leading to highly strategic campaigns that balance customer satisfaction with profitability.

The Bottom Line

Attribution modeling is essential for getting a full view of your digital strategy's performance. By combining rule-based and data-driven approaches, you get the flexibility to analyze each touchpoint's role and the power to adjust with confidence. With attribution, your team isn't guessing where to spend—they're acting on clear insights, avoiding channel conflicts, and building a marketing ecosystem that's greater than the sum of its parts.

AI in All This

AI is like the brains behind the operation in digital analytics, turning mountains of raw data into actionable insights in ways that would be nearly impossible (or at least painfully slow) for a human team. With AI, you're not just collecting data—you're diving into predictive and prescriptive analytics that can spot trends, optimize campaigns, and help make real-time decisions.

At its core, AI in digital analytics streamlines data collection, processing, and analysis, working with everything from structured numbers to the more chaotic world of unstructured data (like social media chatter or customer reviews). Think of it as a tool that reads the room: Machine learning models can tell you which customer segments are most likely to convert, which products are set to fly off the shelves, or even which touchpoints in the customer journey need a little polish.

And AI isn't just looking at numbers; it's processing complex datasets, thanks to tools like natural language processing (NLP) and image recognition. For example, AI can comb through customer reviews to identify sentiment trends, allowing you to spot satisfaction issues early or highlight what customers love. Meanwhile, predictive analytics means you're not just reacting to what's happening now; you're anticipating what's coming. Imagine an AI model that predicts demand spikes based on historical data or social media buzz, letting you adjust inventory and promotions before the trend hits.

By enhancing data quality and reliability, AI ensures you're working with real-time, accurate insights. The best part? AI turns these insights into proactive recommendations, helping your team stay agile, cut costs, and increase impact. In today's fast-paced digital world, AI in analytics isn't just a tech upgrade—it's a game-changer for companies looking to lead the pack.

Key Points

- Digital analytics turns raw data into insights that help businesses understand customer behavior and measure success across areas like sales and marketing.

- Quality and relevance matter. Good data should be accurate, consistent, and relevant to support smart business decisions.
- Focus on the right metrics. Key performance indicators (KPIs) should directly align with business goals to provide clear, actionable insights.
- Big Data needs careful management. Effective tools and data policies keep information secure and ensure it's used responsibly.
- AI boosts analytics by automating data processing, giving predictive insights, and helping businesses react quickly to trends.

As We Move Ahead

Remember, you are analytical, even if you are not the data analyst. You just have those who can run the methods, but you know how to help speak to it and the insights. If you are the analyst, you have the magic wand to build magical insights. Regardless of your role, you all have the collective power to bring data-driven insights to the organization and build effective digital strategies. Now that we have some quantitative reading, let's move to some theory shall we? Be ready for the gray area.

CHAPTER 12

The Gray Area Theory: Embrace It

The important thing is not to stop questioning. Curiosity has its own reason for existing.

—Albert Einstein

Chapter Overview

Albert Einstein highlights the value of curiosity in tackling uncertainty. In digital consumer behavior, curiosity helps marketers explore gray areas— where data are unclear and motivations are complex. This chapter explores how embracing curiosity enables strategists to ask better questions, uncover hidden insights, and create adaptive solutions for evolving consumer needs.

Let's Face It

Digital consumer behavior is a beast of contradictions. One day, your customers are frantically searching for the "best noise-canceling headphones," and the next, they're Googling "do noise-canceling headphones cause loneliness?" It's a digital marketer's rollercoaster, and the track isn't even fully built yet. This is the paradox of the digital consumer—predictable in their unpredictability, consistent in their inconsistency. Welcome to the gray area.

Before you roll your eyes and think, "Great, another vague marketing buzzword," hear me out. The gray area isn't some nebulous concept that exists to complicate your campaign metrics. It's the space between what we know and what we assume—and it's where the magic happens. I claim the theory definition as **the gray area theory** of consumer behavior posits that consumer actions and decisions often occur in ambiguous, uncertain spaces where motivations, influences, and outcomes are not clearly defined, requiring deeper analysis and adaptive strategies to understand and engage effectively.

In this chapter, we'll explore how embracing the gray area in digital consumer behavior can revolutionize your strategy. You'll learn why this space demands curiosity, experimentation, and a willingness to admit that not everything fits neatly into our dashboards. And yes, there will be light humor because, let's be honest, you probably need a laugh after your last campaign review meeting.

The Digital Consumer: A Walking Contradiction

Imagine a shopper named Alex. Alex loves a good bargain and spends hours scouring the Internet for coupon codes. But Alex will also splurge on a premium product if it's marketed as "exclusive" or "limited edition." Alex's behavior doesn't fit neatly into a segment, and that's precisely the point.

Digital consumers like Alex are complex, influenced by a cocktail of emotions, societal norms, and real-time circumstances. They live in the gray area, where:

- **Intent Isn't Always Clear:** Is Alex searching for "best hiking boots" because they're planning a trip or because they want to look outdoorsy on Instagram?
- **Behavior Doesn't Follow Logic:** Why would someone buy a fitness tracker only to ignore every "get moving" notification it sends?
- **Preferences Evolve Constantly:** Today's obsession with plant-based milk could be tomorrow's oat milk fatigue.

Our job isn't to classify Alex as either frugal or indulgent, practical or impulsive. Our job is to embrace the uncertainty and build strategies that thrive in this gray space.

The Gray Area Theory: Redefining Digital Strategy

The Gray Area Theory—yes, I'm trademarking that—is simple yet profound: **Digital consumer behavior doesn't exist in binary.** Forget black and white. Forget "conversion" or "non-conversion." Instead, think gradients, spectrums, and the occasional swirl of chaos.

This theory urges marketers to:

1. **Be Curious:** Ask "why" at least three more times than you normally would. Why did Alex abandon their cart? Why did they click on a competitor's ad? Why are they Googling oat milk recipes at 3 a.m.?
2. **Embrace Ambiguity:** Not every data point needs a definitive answer. Sometimes, a pattern is more valuable than a precise metric.
3. **Experiment Relentlessly:** The gray area is fertile ground for testing new hypotheses. Run A/B tests, tweak your messaging, and don't fear the occasional flop. Failure is just data in disguise.

Curiosity: The Cornerstone of Gray Area Strategy

Curiosity may have killed the cat, but it's also what gave us groundbreaking digital campaigns. When you approach consumer behavior with genuine curiosity, you unlock opportunities others overlook. This is particularly true in the gray area of consumer behavior—those ambiguous spaces where data leave questions unanswered and consumer motivations are nuanced. Success in these spaces requires curiosity, a willingness to explore beyond the obvious, and a mindset that embraces uncertainty as a catalyst for innovation.

Take Spotify's *"Wrapped"* campaign. Instead of focusing solely on listener data, Spotify leaned into the gray area: the emotional connection between music and identity. The result? A campaign that felt personal, playful, and shareable—all because Spotify dared to ask, "What if we let people see themselves through their playlists?" This single question transformed anonymous listening habits into a global phenomenon of self-expression. By exploring how music reflects identity, Spotify turned data into a storytelling opportunity that resonated deeply with its audience.

Curiosity-driven strategies like Spotify's start with asking the right questions. Consider inquiries such as:

• **What emotional need is this consumer trying to meet?**
• **How can we align our brand's story with their personal narrative?**
• **Where are the gaps in their journey, and how can we fill them?**

These questions aren't just about data analysis; they're about understanding the human stories behind the numbers. In the gray area of consumer behavior, emotions, context, and unconscious drivers often matter more than explicit preferences. For instance, a consumer buying luxury skincare may not simply seek high-quality ingredients but validation, self-care, or confidence. A curious marketer would probe deeper, identifying these underlying motivations to craft a campaign that speaks directly to those desires.

The gray area often reveals itself at the intersection of consumer needs and brand purpose. Brands that succeed here embrace the ambiguity, experimenting with messaging, platforms, and interactions to connect authentically. Take Nike's *"You Can't Stop Us"* campaign, which celebrated resilience during the COVID-19 pandemic. By focusing on a universal emotional truth—human determination—Nike bridged cultural differences and created a campaign that resonated globally. This success came from asking, "What unites our audience in this uncertain time?"

Curiosity also plays a crucial role in identifying gaps in the consumer journey. Whether it's a cumbersome checkout process or a lack of personalized recommendations, these gaps represent opportunities for innovation. Amazon excels at this by continuously refining its user experience, addressing gray areas like delivery speed and product discovery to ensure seamless engagement. By asking, "How can we make this experience even better?" Amazon remains ahead of competitors who overlook these nuances.

Ultimately, curiosity in the gray area allows marketers to see opportunities others miss. It shifts the focus from merely solving problems to uncovering potential. Brands that embrace this mindset don't just react to consumer behavior; they shape it. In the digital age, where consumer needs evolve rapidly, curiosity isn't just a trait—it's a necessity.

By exploring the gray area with curiosity, brands can connect with consumers on a deeper level, creating campaigns that are not only memorable but are also transformative. Whether it's turning data into identity, aligning with emotional needs, or addressing journey gaps, curiosity remains the key to unlocking the full potential of digital consumer behavior.

Experimentation: The Playground of the Gray Area

If curiosity is the cornerstone, experimentation is the playground. The gray area in consumer behavior is unpredictable, but it's also rich with potential—if you're willing to get your hands dirty. Experimentation allows marketers to explore uncharted territory, take calculated risks, and uncover new opportunities. It's not about having all the answers upfront but about creating a process to find them.

Consider Netflix's approach to content recommendations. Instead of rigidly categorizing users by broad genres, Netflix experiments with micro-genres like *"Dark Comedies Featuring Strong Female Leads."* This granular approach embraces the nuances of user preferences, tapping into subtle and often overlooked aspects of viewer behavior. By playing in the gray area, Netflix transforms ambiguity into a goldmine of engagement, ensuring its recommendations feel hyper-personalized and relevant.

Effective experimentation in the gray area starts with small, manageable tests. Changing one variable at a time—such as a CTA button color from blue to orange—may seem trivial, but these micro adjustments can yield significant insights over time. Starting small reduces risk, allows for better control over outcomes, and makes it easier to isolate what works. For example, A/B testing is a powerful way to explore consumer reactions without overhauling an entire strategy.

The key to successful experimentation is tracking trends rather than expecting definitive answers. The gray area is inherently fluid, meaning patterns and behaviors often emerge gradually. For instance, a social media campaign might not show immediate success, but tracking engagement over weeks could reveal valuable insights about the audience's preferred content format or posting times. Trends often highlight what works broadly, offering guidance for scaling up initiatives.

Iteration is another vital component of experimentation. Your first experiment is rarely your final answer—it's just the beginning. Even inconclusive results can inform the next steps by showing what didn't resonate. For example, when Spotify introduced its Discover Weekly playlist, early iterations weren't perfect. However, through continuous refinement, Spotify learned how to blend algorithmic data with human curation, creating one of its most beloved features. Experimentation isn't about perfection; it's about progress.

The gray area requires a mindset that values learning over immediate results. Brands that embrace experimentation thrive by asking, "What if?" and following the trail wherever it leads. Take Airbnb, for instance. Early on, the company faced a challenge in attracting hosts. Through small experiments, such as offering free photography services for listings, Airbnb discovered that high-quality photos significantly increased bookings. This insight shaped their long-term strategy, demonstrating how simple experiments can lead to transformative outcomes.

Experimentation in the gray area also fosters innovation by encouraging teams to challenge assumptions. What if your audience responds better to humor than professionalism? What if shifting your e-mail subject line from formal to conversational increases open rates? By testing these hypotheses, brands can break free from outdated practices and adapt to evolving consumer preferences.

Ultimately, experimentation turns the uncertainty of the gray area into a playground of possibilities. It's a cycle of testing, learning, and iterating that allows marketers to uncover hidden opportunities, refine their strategies, and stay ahead in an ever-changing digital landscape. Just as Netflix redefined content recommendations and Airbnb revolutionized hospitality, brands willing to experiment in the gray area can unlock groundbreaking solutions and drive meaningful engagement.

Discovery and Intent: Navigating the Consumer Journey

In the gray area of consumer behavior, discovery and intent rarely follow a straight path. A consumer might encounter your brand by chance while exploring unrelated interests, or they might have intent buried beneath hesitation, distractions, or competing priorities. Understanding and navigating these nuances is key to turning passive curiosity into active engagement.

Picture a consumer researching *"best dog-friendly travel destinations"* who lands on your website. They're not ready to book a trip; they're just gathering ideas. This moment of discovery is your opportunity to nurture them—not through aggressive sales tactics but by creating a connection that keeps your brand top of mind. Success lies in meeting the consumer where they are, even if their intent isn't immediate.

One effective strategy is offering **content that educates and entertains.** For a consumer exploring dog-friendly travel, blog posts detailing pet-friendly hotels, how-to videos about traveling with pets, or interactive quizzes like "What's Your Ideal Dog-Friendly Getaway?" provide immediate value. This type of content builds trust while subtly guiding the consumer toward your offerings without pressuring them to convert right away.

Another approach is **retargeting that respects the gray area.** Retargeting campaigns often bombard users with ads urging them to act, but a more nuanced approach works better in the gray area. Instead of direct sales pitches, gentle reminders—such as an ad showcasing a heartwarming story about a traveler and their dog—keep the consumer engaged. These subtle touchpoints maintain relevance without overwhelming the consumer, leaving room for them to progress in their journey naturally.

Personalization with a light touch is also essential for navigating discovery and intent. Use consumer data to anticipate their needs, but avoid being overly prescriptive. For instance, if a user browses your site's travel guides, recommending additional resources like packing lists or destination tips shows attentiveness without being intrusive. This balance respects the consumer's autonomy and leaves space for unexpected behaviors or interests to emerge.

Discovery and intent in the gray area require brands to think beyond immediate conversions and embrace long-term relationship-building. By understanding that intent can be fluid and discovery often serendipitous, marketers can develop strategies that nurture consumers at every stage of their journey. Whether through engaging content, thoughtful retargeting, or flexible personalization, brands that navigate this space effectively position themselves as trusted partners in the consumer's decision-making process.

The gray area isn't a barrier; it's an opportunity to meet consumers where they are, offer meaningful value, and build connections that outlast any single transaction. By focusing on discovery and intent with curiosity and empathy, brands can transform fleeting interest into enduring loyalty.

The Humor of It All: Finding Joy in the Gray

Let's admit it: Working in digital marketing can sometimes feel like chasing a moving target while blindfolded. The constant shifts in consumer behavior, technology, and trends can be daunting—but they can also be a lot of fun. The gray area, with all its unpredictability, isn't just a challenge; it's an open invitation to innovate, laugh, and connect in ways that defy traditional strategies.

Take a page from brands like Wendy's, whose Twitter strategy thrives in the gray area of sass and spontaneity. Rather than sticking to safe, polished messaging, Wendy's leans into unpredictability, roasting competitors and responding to fans with humor and wit. This bold, playful approach has transformed a fast-food chain into a social media icon, proving that embracing the chaos of the gray area can yield unexpected rewards.

The beauty of humor in the gray area lies in its ability to humanize a brand. When marketers let go of rigid formulas and embrace spontaneity, they create moments that feel genuine and relatable. These moments resonate with audiences because they reflect the messiness of real life—a far cry from the perfectly curated ads consumers are used to.

Remember, the gray area isn't just a space for solving problems; it's a playground for creativity. Whether it's experimenting with a quirky tone, launching an offbeat campaign, or simply having fun with your audience, humor can turn ambiguity into opportunity. By finding joy in the gray, you not only navigate uncertainty but thrive in it, creating experiences that audiences will remember and share.

Conclusion: The Case for Staying Curious

The gray area isn't a problem to be solved—it's a space to be explored. It demands curiosity, patience, and a willingness to embrace the unknown. It's where discovery and intent overlap, where data meet intuition and where creativity thrives.

As practitioners, our job isn't to eliminate the gray area. It's to live in it, learn from it, and leverage it to create strategies that resonate. So, let's stop chasing absolutes and start embracing the gradients. After all, the best campaigns aren't black and white—they're a beautiful shade of gray.

Key Points

- The gray area is where consumer behavior is unpredictable and requires adaptive strategies.
- Curiosity helps uncover opportunities by exploring emotional connections.
- Experimentation reveals preferences through small, iterative tests.
- Discovery and intent are nurtured with content, retargeting, and personalization.
- Humor and creativity turn ambiguity into memorable connections.

As We Move Ahead

Feeling curious yet? Empowered to explore? Well good. We have one final chapter to embrace the future of digital consumer behavior, specifically, in the aspect of new technology and the changing landscape of digital business.

CHAPTER 13

Future Trends: The AI and Advanced Tech Paradigm

Tell me and I forget. Teach me and I remember. Involve me and I learn.

—*Benjamin Franklin*

Chapter Overview

Benjamin Franklin's wisdom rings true in the age of gamification. Brands today know that involvement is key. Instead of just telling consumers about a product or teaching them its benefits, gamification pulls people into an interactive experience. Think of a fitness app that rewards your workouts with badges or a shopping site that turns browsing into a playful adventure. By engaging users in fun, meaningful ways, brands ensure the message sticks, making each interaction memorable and exciting. Franklin was right—getting involved makes all the difference.

The New Abyss

Now as we enter the late 2020s, into the 2030s and beyond, we are approaching what can only be described as a "new abyss" of digital consumption. This isn't a transition in and of itself; it's a coming revolution that is as exciting as it is terrifying. Technology is changing at lightning speed and so is the way consumers interact, choose, even experience reality in ways we're only now coming to terms with. From hyper-personalized algorithms and AR (augmented reality) and VR (virtual reality)–driven shopping to disconnected on- and offline worlds, the online experience is becoming more dense, immersive, and volatile than ever.

The new world presents us with immense opportunities and overwhelming threats. On the one hand, AI-based behavioral analytics and omnichannel integrations offer customers new opportunities for engagement. Brands are able to anticipate needs, personalize interactions real-time, and forge connections that are almost mystical in their relevance. Yet the very technologies that promise to improve our lives also elicit questions about privacy, data ethics, and the psychological effects of digital addiction. Trust is one of the most precious and unstable currencies of the digital era as consumers become more aware of what happens with their data—and misuse it.

Going forward, this era will require a different sort of digital wisdom. Firms will need to become the leaders of responsible innovation and balance the promise of consumer intelligence with ethical action. Meanwhile, consumers will need to get used to a world in which digital footprints define their experience more than ever before. This section examines the new black hole we're about to dive into, how the digital consumer is being radically transformed, what is creating these disruptions, and how brands will have to make do in order to survive, let alone thrive in this new world.

Hyper-Personalization Through Advanced AI

Remember when personalization meant just slapping someone's first name on an e-mail and calling it a day? Those times are as outdated as a flip phone in a world of foldables. Today, it's all about hyper-personalization, and we have advanced AI to thank for that. Brands are no longer just trying to guess what you like; they're practically reading your mind. Or, at least, they're getting eerily close.

Here's the scoop: AI-powered algorithms can now sift through mind-boggling amounts of data to figure out not only your preferences but also your behaviors, mood, and even what's going on in the outside world. It's like your favorite brand has been studying you more intently than a dog eyeballing your dinner plate. The goal? To deliver the right content to the right person at the *perfect* moment. Think of it as the digital equivalent of your best friend magically showing up with a cup of coffee right when you need it most.

Take streaming services, for instance. They're not just recommending shows you might enjoy based on your past binges. Oh no, they're now taking into account whether it's raining outside or if you just watched a heart-wrenching drama (because clearly, you need a pick-me-up). Hyper-personalization means these services get so specific, you'll feel like the universe is watching out for you—unless, of course, it starts recommending rom-coms at 2 a.m. when you're trying to work. In that case, maybe it's watching you *too* closely.

Why does this matter? Because our attention spans are shrinking faster than those jeans you put in the dryer by mistake. Consumers want instant gratification. If a brand's message misses the mark, it's "Bye, Felicia." Hyper-personalization is the key to keeping us hooked. Companies that get it right see higher engagement, more conversions, and a fan base that sticks around. The flipside? It's a pricey game. Rolling out hyper-personalization means serious investment in AI and some heavy-duty data infrastructure. Oh, and don't even get me started on the data privacy concerns. People don't love it when a brand knows them *too* well. There's a fine line between being helpful and creeping people out.

The future, though? It's going to be wild. AI and machine learning are getting smarter by the minute, and the possibilities are endless. Imagine your favorite retail app restocking your pantry before you even notice you're low on coffee. Or your smartwatch creating custom wellness plans based on your heart rate and activity. We're heading into a world where our digital and physical experiences blend so seamlessly, your gadgets might just know what you need before you do.

So, whether you're excited or a little nervous, one thing is certain: Hyper-personalization is here to stay, and it's making the digital world as tailored to you as your favorite pair of socks. (Assuming you wear socks that actually match, of course.)

Behavioral Biometrics: A New Data Frontier

As digital consumers—aka *all of us*—get more complex and demanding, the methods companies use to understand us are getting equally advanced. Enter behavioral biometrics: a game-changer that uses unique physical and behavioral traits to decode consumer actions and intentions. We're talking about things like the way you type, the rhythm of your mouse movements, or even the delicate way you swipe your smartphone screen. Yes, even your phone knows when you're feeling a bit indecisive.

Imagine this: You're browsing an e-commerce site, eyeing that overpriced-but-probably-worth-it gadget. Behavioral biometrics is working behind the scenes, tracking how long you hover over the product, how fast you scroll, and whether your scrolling pace screams "just browsing" or "seriously tempted." If the system detects hesitation—maybe your mouse movement slows or you start scrolling nervously—it could suggest a discount or pop up a friendly, *non-annoying* chat offer. Basically, it's like the online version of a helpful salesperson who magically appears when you need them (but without the awkward small talk).

What makes behavioral biometrics so revolutionary? Well, it doesn't just help companies figure out who's truly engaged versus who's scrolling absentmindedly while watching TV. It also takes security up a notch. With cyberthreats looming larger than ever, using these behavioral patterns for authentication is a serious step forward. Passwords can be hacked or stolen, but replicating the way someone taps, swipes, or types? Now, *that's* tough. It's like trying to mimic someone's signature dance move—you can try, but you'll probably fail.

Of course, like your nosiest aunt at Thanksgiving, this tech comes with a lot of baggage. The main concern? Privacy. Sure, it's cool to get personalized experiences, but do we really want companies keeping tabs on every scroll, click, and swipe? And if data breaches are bad now, imagine the fallout if someone leaks your biometric data. There's no changing your behavioral patterns the way you'd change a password (unless you suddenly learn to type like a T-Rex).

This is why transparency is crucial. If businesses want to use this tech, they better come clean about what's being tracked, why, and how securely it's being stored. Clear, upfront consumer consent and airtight data protection policies will make or break the trust game. Nobody wants to feel like they're part of a creepy science experiment, even if the end goal is to create seamless, secure experiences.

Looking ahead, it's clear that behavioral biometrics will play a bigger role, especially in industries like banking and e-commerce. We're on the brink of a world where everyday interactions come with hyper-relevant, ultra-secure personalization. But as this trend accelerates, companies must juggle innovation with consumer trust. Because let's face it, even the most cutting-edge tech won't fly if it leaves us feeling more watched than impressed.

The Rise of Emotion AI

Alright, let's get into the fascinating world of Emotion AI, or as it's fancily known, affective computing. Marketers have always dreamed of understanding our feelings—without the guesswork. Enter Emotion AI, which uses facial recognition, natural language processing, and sentiment analysis to read our emotions like an open book. It's a bit like having a digital empath that knows when we're on the verge of a meltdown or ready to impulse-buy that pair of shoes.

Picture this: You're dealing with a frustrating chatbot that makes you question your life choices. If that bot detects the growing irritation in your text or tone, it could call in human backup faster than you can say "customer service nightmare." Or imagine a digital ad that changes on the fly based on whether you're smiling or scowling. The goal? To make you feel seen, understood, and, ideally, not annoyed.

Consumers today want brands that "get them," and Emotion AI delivers on that desire for real connections. From customer service to digital advertising, emotion-driven tech adds a touch of empathy. And let's be honest, a brand that makes us feel valued is one we're more likely to trust, engage with, and stick around for.

But hold up—there are some red flags. Emotion AI isn't perfect. What if it misreads a neutral expression as angry or gets privacy all wrong? Do we really want our emotions constantly analyzed? Clear ethical guidelines and transparency are key to making sure this tech doesn't cross the line from helpful to downright creepy.

Going forward, expect Emotion AI to keep evolving, with smarter algorithms and (hopefully) better rules. Brands that use it wisely will win hearts—and consumer loyalty—in a whole new way.

The Evolution of Social Commerce

Platforms like Instagram, TikTok, and Pinterest aren't just for cat videos and photo dumps anymore. Nope, they've become legit shopping hubs where you can discover, shop, and share products in one seamless experience. It's a whole new world, driven by social media's power to shape our shopping habits.

So, what's the deal? Social commerce blends social media and e-commerce, letting you buy that must-have jacket or trending gadget without leaving the app you're already scrolling. Brands are taking advantage by posting shoppable content, tapping into influencer marketing, and even running live shopping events to keep us engaged (and spending). The best part? Younger generations are totally here for it, spending a lot of their time—and money—based on social inspiration.

Speaking of influencers, they're the secret sauce of social commerce. Let's be real: Most of us are way more likely to trust a skincare tip from our favorite TikToker than from a random ad. Brands that build genuine connections with influencers see a major boost in visibility and trustworthiness. It's influencer marketing 2.0, and it's only getting bigger.

And then there's live shopping—think of it as QVC for the TikTok generation. It's an interactive experience where you can ask questions, see demos, and make purchases in real-time. It's like window shopping but with fewer steps and more impulsive buying (oops).

Of course, it's not all sunshine and viral sales. Brands have to strike the right balance between promoting products and engaging authentically. Overdo it, and you risk giving your audience a serious case of ad fatigue. Plus, making shopping smooth across all these platforms is a logistical headache.

What's next? Expect even tighter integration between content and shopping, with new features like AR-based try-ons and gamified shopping. The future of social commerce is fun, interactive, and all about keeping up with the fast-moving digital communities that make it thrive.

Gamification and Interactive Experiences

Let's talk about gamification. You know, the concept that turns everyday tasks into something fun and rewarding—kind of like giving yourself a gold star for doing adult things, like going to the gym or remembering to pay your bills on time. Gamification is becoming a major strategy for brands, and it's not just about making things fun (though that's a big part of it); it's also a brilliant way to gather consumer data while keeping engagement levels high.

So, why does this work so well? Humans are naturally competitive and love a good reward. Whether it's scoring points or unlocking badges or leveling up, gamification taps into our psychological desire for accomplishment. Think about it: A fitness app that rewards you for hitting your daily step count can make getting off the couch feel like a major victory. Retailers use this strategy to hook consumers too. Remember when you collected points for every purchase and raced to earn that sweet 20-percent-off coupon? Yep, that's gamification in action.

But it's not just about the thrill of the game. There's a serious side to gamification—*data collection*. Every time you interact with a gamified experience, you're giving brands insights into your preferences and behavior. If you're always participating in quizzes about skincare or competing in online challenges about meal planning, brands learn what makes you tick and can tailor their marketing strategies to meet your needs. It's like spying, but more fun and less creepy (hopefully).

The potential for this is enormous, but let's be real: Not all gamified experiences are winners. Ever tried a gamified app that felt like a complete waste of time or a loyalty program so complicated you gave up? That's what happens when gamification goes wrong. If the experience feels gimmicky or forced, consumers check out fast. It's critical for brands to ensure that these game-like elements serve a purpose and provide actual value. Nobody wants to earn "useless badge #57" for visiting a website five times, especially if there's no real reward.

Challenges aside, the future of gamification is seriously exciting. As AR (Augmented Reality) and VR (Virtual Reality) become more mainstream, we'll see immersive experiences that blur the lines between reality and the digital world. Imagine an AR treasure hunt where you collect digital prizes at your favorite stores or a VR shopping experience that feels like a videogame. The goal? Make your interactions with a brand so engaging that you forget you're being marketed to.

Social engagement is also a massive part of where gamification is headed. Multiplayer experiences, where you and your friends can team up or compete, are likely to become more popular. Brands are figuring out that we love sharing these moments, whether it's bragging about beating our friend in a virtual game or collaborating on a digital challenge. These social elements make the experience richer and more memorable.

And let's not forget about *personalization*. As AI and data analytics continue to advance, brands will be able to tailor gamified experiences to your specific interests and habits. Imagine a workout app that adjusts its challenges based on your fitness level or a shopping site that gamifies your product search based on what you've bought before. It's like having a personal game designer who knows exactly how to keep you entertained—and spending, of course.

The key to long-term success with gamification is balance. It's not just about making things fun; it's about making things meaningful. The experience should feel rewarding in a way that adds real value, whether that's saving money, learning something new, or feeling more motivated to reach your goals. When done right, gamification can turn passive consumers into active participants, fostering loyalty that keeps people coming back for more.

So, where does this leave us? In a world where experiences are becoming more interactive, brands need to stay innovative and agile. The gamification trend is not going anywhere, and it's evolving quickly. From personalized game mechanics to social, immersive AR adventures, the future is full of possibilities. If brands can master the art of making their interactions genuinely engaging and rewarding, they'll have consumers playing along happily—and that's a win for everyone.

Key Points

- The "new abyss" is a digital revolution blending hyper-personalization, AR, and immersive experiences in a dense, fast-evolving online world.
- New tech lets brands deliver real-time personalized experiences but raises concerns about privacy, ethics, and digital addiction.
- Trust is fragile as consumers grow more aware and cautious of how their data are used.

- Companies must balance innovation with ethical practices to stay relevant in this shifting landscape.
- Consumers' digital footprints will shape their experiences more than ever, demanding greater awareness and adaptability.

Until We Meet Again

First, thank you. You took the time to absorb this modern view of digital consumer behavior, and the goal of learning innovative and emerging trends, technologies, and methods to compete in your industry. Remember, your company and industry are unique, so it's not a one-size-fits-all with all of these factors discussed in this book. You need to find the things that stick, and when they stick, keep them sticky. Continue to test and innovate. You learn by doing. You succeed by failing. Take risks, but, more importantly, calculated risks.

I have seen the good, the bad, and the ugly, as I have expressed throughout this book. The ugly was not so much the final results of a failed digital strategy to engage and convert online consumers. The ugly was the internal culture not embracing technology, trends, or advances in consumer behavior. It left me craving for the environment to thrive in. When I got to those environments, I saw the good and then the great in the results.

So, go be your own digital consumer behavior steward now. Take what you may have been inspired by and run with it and make it your own. By the way, you saw a lot of quotes in this book right? Let me leave you with one more, the most profound quote I have always used as my mission in digital business:

A limit is a myth created by those not willing to try new things
—Anonymous

Bibliography

Ajzen, I. 1991. "The Theory of Planned Behavior." *Organizational Behavior and Human Decision Processes* 50 (2): 179–211.

Bandura, A. 1971. *Social Learning Theory*. New York: General Learning Press.

Bishop, A. 2021. "The 6 Most Important PPC KPIs You Should Be Tracking." *Search Engine Journal*, May 3. https://www.searchenginejournal.com/ppc-guide/most-important-ppc-kpis/#close.

Bond Brand Loyalty. 2023. "The Loyalty Report 2023."

Capgemini. (2017). *The disconnected customer: What digital customer experience leaders teach us about reconnecting with customers*. Capgemini Digital Transformation Institute. https://www.capgemini.com/co-es/wp-content/uploads/sites/28/2022/12/the_disconnected_customer-what_digital_customer_experience_leaders_teach_us_about_reconnecting_with_customers.pdf

Capital One Shopping. 2024. "Online Review Statistics (2024): Influence on Buying Decisions."

Cisco. (2022). *2022 Consumer Privacy Survey*. https://investor.cisco.com/news/news-details/2022/Consumers-want-more-transparency-on-how-businesses-handle-their-data-new-Cisco-survey-shows/default.aspx

Cuddy, A. J. C., M. Kohut, and J. Neffinger. 2013. "Connect, Then Lead." *Harvard Business Review* 91 (7/8): 54–61.

Deloitte. 2024. "Digital Consumer Trends UK 2024: Generative AI." *Wall Street Journal*. https://www.deloitte.com/uk/en/Industries/tmt/research/digital-consumer-trends-2024-gen-ai.html.

Dooley, Roger. 2012. *Brainfluence: 100 Ways to Persuade and Convince Consumers with Neuromarketing*. Wiley.

Dun & Bradstreet. (2022, September 2). *Corporate Policy Statement: Privacy and Personal Data Protection*. https://www.dnb.com/content/dam/web/company/about/content/ppdp/DnB_Privacy-and-Personal-Data-Protection-Policy-Statement-Tier-1-CP-5.pdf

Dunning, D., and J. Kruger. 1999. "Unskilled and Unaware of It: How Difficulties in Recognizing One's Own Incompetence Lead to Inflated Self-Assessments." *Journal of Personality and Social Psychology* 77 (6): 1121–34.

Edge Delta. 2024, March 8. "Eye-opening Data Analytics Statistics for 2024." Edge Delta. https://edgedelta.com/company/blog/data-analytics-statistics.

EMARKETER. 2020. "Digital Buyers Worldwide, 2020–2025 (Billions, % Change, and % of Population)." https://www.emarketer.com/chart/253520/digital-buyers-worldwide-2020-2025-billions-change-of-population.

Exploding Topics. 2025. "Internet Traffic from Mobile Devices (Feb 2025)." *Exploding Topics*, May 16, 2025. https://explodingtopics.com/blog/mobile-internet-traffic.

Filieri, R., L. Zollo, R. Rialti, and S. Yoon. 2021. "Brand Betrayal, Post-purchase Regret, and Consumer Responses to Service Failures: A comparison Between Utilitarian and Hedonic Products." *Journal of Business Research* 132, 799–812. https://doi.org/10.1016/j.jbusres.2021.04.025

Firework. 2025. "69.57% of Online Shoppers Leave without Purchasing: Shocking 50+ Cart Abandonment Statistics." *Firework Blog*, February 25, 2025. https://www.firework.com/blog/cart-abandonment-statistics.

Forrester. 2023. "Define the Right Metrics for Tracking CRM Success." July 27. https://www.forrester.com/report/define-the-right-metrics-for-tracking-crm-success/RES59408.

Gartner. 2024a. "Insights on AI in Marketing." https://www.gartner.com/en/marketing/topics/ai-in-marketing.

Gartner. 2024b. "Prepare for the Future of AI-Powered Customers."

Google. 2016. "The Need for Mobile Speed." *Marketing Dive*. https://www.marketingdive.com/news/google-53-of-mobile-users-abandon-sites-that-take-over-3-seconds-to-load/426070/.

Greathouse, John. 2013. "5 Time-Tested Success Tips from Amazon Founder Jeff Bezos." *Forbes*, April 30. https://www.forbes.com/sites/johngreathouse/2013/04/30/5-time-tested-success-tips-from-amazon-founder-jeff-bezos/.

Harvard Business Review. (2016, August 29). An emotional connection matters more than customer satisfaction. https://hbr.org/2016/08/an-emotional-connection-matters-more-than-customer-satisfaction

Haynes, T. 2023. "Define Effective Digital Marketing KPIs to Achieve Your Goals." *Smart Insights*, March 15. https://www.smartinsights.com/goal-setting-evaluation/goals-kpis/choosing-effective-digital-marketing-kpis/.

Heskett, J. L., W. E. Sasser, and L. A. Schlesinger. 1994. "The Service Profit Chain." *Harvard Business Review*.

Heider, F. 1946. "Attitudes and Cognitive Organization." *Journal of Psychology*, 21, 107–12.

Holistic SEO. 2023. "45 FOMO Statistics, Facts, and Trends." August 22. https://www.holisticseo.digital/marketing/statistic/fomo.

Hootsuite. 2023. "Digital 2023: Global Overview Report." https://www.hootsuite.com/resources/digital-trends.

HubSpot. 2017. "What Do 76% of Consumers Want from Your Website? New Data." *HubSpot Blog*, July 28, 2017. https://blog.hubspot.com/blog/tabid/6307/bid/14953/what-do-76-of-consumers-want-from-your-website-new-data.aspx.

HubSpot. 2022, January 12. "How to Ask & Get Good Customer Reviews [+Examples]." https://blog.hubspot.com/service/get-customer-reviews.

Intelligence Node. 2024. "The 2024 Consumer Behavior Trends: 40 Stats for Retail Success." https://www.intelligencenode.com/resources/consumer-buying-behavior-report-2024.

Invoca. 2025. "Data-Driven Marketing Trends for 2025: Why You Need to Update Your Strategy." *Invoca.com*, March 4, 2025. https://www.invoca.com/blog/state-of-data-driven-marketing-update-your-strategy.

Kemp, Simon. 2024. "Digital 2024—An In-Depth Report Analysis." *Meltwater*, January 31. https://www.meltwater.com/en/blog/digital-2024.

Kotler, P. 2016. *Marketing Management*. 15th ed. Pearson.

King-Hill, S. 2015. "Critical Analysis of Maslow's Hierarchy of Need." *The STeP Journal (Student Teacher Perspectives)* 2(4): 54–57. https://insight.cumbria.ac.uk/id/eprint/2942/1/KingHill_CriticalAnalysisOfMaslows.pdf.

Leggett, K. 2023. "Define the Right Metrics for Tracking CRM Success." *Forrester*, July 27. https://www.forrester.com/report/define-the-right-metrics-for-tracking-crm-success/RES59408.

Lindstrom, Martin. 2010. *Buyology: Truth and Lies About Why We Buy*. Crown Business.

Maslow, A. H. 1970. *Motivation and Personality*. 2nd ed. Harper & Row.

McKinsey & Company. 2024a. "How Generative AI Can Boost Consumer Marketing." https://www.mckinsey.com/capabilities/growth-marketing-and-sales/our-insights/how-generative-ai-can-boost-consumer-marketing.

McKinsey & Company. 2024b. "The Next Frontier of Customer Engagement: AI-Enabled Customer Service." https://www.mckinsey.com/capabilities/operations/our-insights/the-next-frontier-of-customer-engagement-ai-enabled-customer-service.

McKnight, D. H., and N. L. Chervany. 2001. "Trust and Distrust Definitions: One Bite at a Time." In *Trust in Cyber-Societies,* edited by R. Falcone, M. Singh, and Y. H. Tan. Lecture Notes in Computer Science, vol. 2246. Springer.

McKinsey & Company. 2023, May 30. "What Is Personalization?" https://www.mckinsey.com/featured-insights/mckinsey-explainers/what-is-personalization.

Meyer, C., and A. Schwager. 2007. "Understanding Customer Experience." *Harvard Business Review*.

MoEngage. 2023. "51 Mind-Blowing Mobile Marketing Statistics and Trends for 2023."

Moran, Gillian, Laurent Muzellec, and Eoghan Nolan. 2014. "Consumer Moments of Truth in the Digital Context." *Journal of Advertising Research* 54 (2): 200–4.

Motista. 2018. *Leveraging the Value of Emotional Connection for Retailers* [White Paper]. Motista, Inc. https://inspirefire.com/wp-content/uploads/2019/08/3.3 _Motista_Leveraging-Emotional-Connection-for-Retailers.pdf.

Narver, J. C., and S. F. Slater. 1990. "The Effect of a Market Orientation on Business Profitability." *Journal of Marketing* 54 (4): 20–35.

NIQ Consumer Outlook. 2024. "Consumer Outlook 2024: 6 Consumer Sentiment-Driven Strategies to Drive Growth and Capture Spending." *NIQ*.

Omol, R. 2023. "Digital Transformation as a Catalyst for Business Model Innovation." *Open Access Research Journal of Engineering and Technology* 3(4): 1–22. https://oarjpublication.com/journals/oarjet/sites/default/files /OARJET-2023-0085.pdf.

Pavlov, I. P. 1927. *Conditioned Reflexes: An Investigation of the Physiological Activity of the Cerebral Cortex.* London: Oxford University Press.

Pearse, N. 2014. "Service as a Required Leadership Competency." Presented at the Proceedings of the 10th European Conference on Management Leadership and Governance, Vern University of Applied Science, Zagreb, Republic of Croatia, November 2014.

Pew Research Center. 2019. "Americans Are Wary of the Role Social Media Sites Play in Delivering the News." *Pew Research Center*, October 2, 2019. https:// www.pewresearch.org/journalism/2019/10/02/americans-are-wary-of-the-role-social-media-sites-play-in-delivering-the-news/.

Pew Research Center. 2023. "How Americans View Data Privacy." *Pew Research Center*, October 18, 2023. https://www.pewresearch.org/internet/2023/10/18 /how-americans-view-data-privacy/.

Phillips, J. 2016. *Ecommerce Analytics: Analyze and Improve the Impact of Your Digital Strategy.* Amazon. https://www.amazon.com/Ecommerce -Analytics-Analyze-Improve-Strategy/dp/0134177282.

Porter, Britney. 2023. "How Leveraging Data Can Enhance Your Business Success." *Forbes*, September 14. https://www.forbes.com/sites/britneyporter/2023/09/14 /how-leveraging-data-can-enhance-your-business-success/.

PowerReviews. 2023. "Survey: The Ever-Growing Power of Reviews (2023 Edition)." https://www.powerreviews.com.

Sprout Social. 2023. "The Sprout Social Index, Edition XVII: Accelerate." https:// sproutsocial.com/insights/data/social-media-trends.

Termly. 2025, January 24. "64 Alarming Data Privacy Statistics Businesses Must See in 2025." https://termly.io/resources/articles/data-privacy-statistics/.

Thales Group. 2024. "2024 Data Security Directions Council Report." https:// cpl.thalesgroup.com/resources/2024-data-security-directions-council-report.

Think with Google. 2016, July. "How Mobile Has Redefined the Consumer Decision Journey for Shoppers." https://think.storage.googleapis.com/docs /mobile-redefined-consumer-decision-shopper-journey.pdf.

Tschohl, J. 2020. "Treat Customers Like Life-Long Partners." *Agency Sales* 50 (6): 46–48.

Tversky, Amos, and Daniel Kahneman. 1981. "The Framing of Decisions and the Psychology of Choice." *Science* 211 (4481): 453–58.

Wong, J. C. 2019. "The Cambridge Analytica Scandal Changed the World—But It Didn't Change Facebook." *Guardian*, March 18. https://www.theguardian .com/technology/2019/mar/17/the-cambridge-analytica-scandal-changed -the-world-but-it-didnt-change-facebook.

Zorfas, Alan, and Daniel Leemon. 2016. "An Emotional Connection Matters More Than Customer Satisfaction." *Harvard Business Review*, August 29. https://hbr .org/2016/08/an-emotional-connection-matters-more-than-customer-satisfaction.

About the Author

Dr. Kyle Allison is known as The Doctor of Digital Strategy. He is an accomplished author, business and marketing professor, and senior executive in the e-commerce and digital marketing industry. Having worked for leading organizations in the retail sector, Dr. Allison has driven high-impact digital strategies, leading initiatives in technology, marketing campaigns, e-commerce experiences, and more. His professional philosophy centers on enthusiasm, education, and excellence, integrating these values into every pillar of his academic and business career.

With extensive experience teaching digital marketing, analytics, management, and business subjects, Dr. Allison has developed and led academic programs and taught at all educational levels, including doctoral. He also has served as a DBA doctoral chair, where he is dedicated to mentoring the next generation of business scholars and professionals.

Dr. Allison's publications include Quick Study Guides, textbooks on Digital Marketing, Digital Analytics, and E-commerce, which combine scholarly insight with hands-on executive experience. In addition he has written professional trade books for executive audience in these topics. His writing emphasizes practical application, ensuring that the material not only meets academic learning outcomes but also translates effectively to real-world scenarios.

Dr. Kyle Allison holds a DBA, MS, MBA, and BA, all with a focus on business leadership and communication.

For more information about Dr. Kyle Allison's publications, C.V., and services, visit DoctorofDigitalStrategy.com.

Index